Becoming a Better Friend

MELODIE M. DAVIS

Becoming a Better Friend

MELODIE M. DAVIS

BETHANY HOUSE PUBLISHERS
MINNEAPOLIS, MINNESOTA 55438
A Division of Bethany Fellowship, Inc.

Copyright © 1988
Melodie M. Davis
All Rights Reserved

Published by Bethany House Publishers
A Division of Bethany Fellowship, Inc.
6820 Auto Club Road, Minneapolis, Minnesota 55438

Printed in the United States of America

Library of Congress Cataloging-in-Publication Data

Davis, Melodie M., 1951–
  Becoming a better friend.

   1. Friendship. 2. Conduct of life. I. Title.
BJ1533.F8D384   1988   177'.6   88–19455
ISBN 1-55661-001-7   CIP

My husband, my friend

MELODIE M. DAVIS is a staff writer for the Mennonite Board of Missions Media Ministries and writes programs and promotional materials. She is the author of two books with Zondervan and one book with Word. She is married and their family includes three girls.

ACKNOWLEDGMENTS

Much of the material in this book comes from scripts I wrote for the *Your Time* radio program hosted by friend and co-worker Margaret Foth. Thanks to Paul Yoder, Lowell Hertzler, Ken Weaver and Pam Beverage for guidance and advice on shaping it into a book.

A special thanks to Marian Bauman, assistant; Diane Deviers, typist; Patty Eckard, proofreader; and Nathan Unseth, editor at Bethany House Publishers. Finally, thanks to all of the wonderful people at Trinity Presbyterian Church, friends and family for their contributions—implicit or explicit—in the illustrations they've provided for this book.

CONTENTS

INTRODUCTION

I've never been the life of any party. In fact, I've spent a great many parties envying the person whose every joke went over to rave reviews, whose hair always bounced, and whose mouthwash always worked.

On the home front I'm not exactly up for any friendly-person-of-the-year awards either. I've been known to pout, rant and otherwise make life difficult—first for my parents, then roommates, and now my husband, children and dog. So what could possibly qualify me to write a book on becoming someone people love to be around?

That's exactly the point. A book on how to get along with people shouldn't be written by someone who has no trouble being the life of the party. Charisma comes so effortlessly to those kinds of people that they probably couldn't begin to tell you why people like them. These few blessed people (and you will meet some of them in this book) receive their charm as a gift from God, plain and simple. They are so likeable you can't even be jealous of them. So a book on how to be a friend needs to be written by someone who's still in the process of learning.

Second, this is a layperson's book: It isn't a psychological treatise on personality, nor a scientific explanation on how deodorant works. It is simply reflections, learned through some thirty-odd years of reading, chatting and researching—and, like I said, through a lot of observations scanned from my standard place decorating the wall. Each chapter starts by examining a problem and a superficial "answer," goes on to explore the deeper levels of what it takes to be open to people, and concludes with several specific tips.

A lot of times we wish we could change the people we relate to, but this book concentrates on changing the only person I can really change—myself. If this book is used in a group, members might promise one another to try a certain number of exercises given at the end of each chapter. Some of the ideas aren't new—you've tried them before—but if you're really serious about growing in relationships, I hope you'll be challenged to actively try some new steps. You may never be considered the life of the party, but by implementing some of these steps you'll learn to like yourself better.

Writing this book has been hard. Putting the ideas down on paper and making them presentable was not as difficult as having to face the reality that I still am not, nor probably ever will be, the world's friendliest person. This project has stretched me to continue in my efforts to grow in this area. I know, thankfully, that "God's grace is sufficient for me." I want to be a better friend—not just to make me a nicer, more popular person, but because God wants to draw others to the kingdom through me—*and* you.

SOME PEOPLE ARE SO NICE, YOU CAN'T EVEN BE JEALOUS OF THEM

CHAPTER ONE

I always hated the advice I heard from well-intentioned people when I was growing up: "If you want to have friends, you have to be friendly." Of course, what my teachers, guidance counselors and youth group sponsors spoke was sensible wisdom, taken straight from that wonderfully sound verse in Prov. 18:24.

Why did this kind of advice make me arch my back like a cat suddenly wary? Because it went against the grain of my personality. I was always sort of a loner who wandered around our home farm writing poetry and belting out operatic arias to the ever-attentive cows. I was the only girl in my high school gang of about eight friends who never took her turn having a slumber party. Why? Our house was quite adequate, my family more than accepting of friends and even all-night noise. I guess I just worried that no one would have fun.

And that is the crux of the matter: We are often afraid to reach out in friendship for fear of being rejected. We fear not being accepted, or that no one will laugh at our jokes. And it is that very worrying about *self* that alienates others from us.

I'll never forget a woman I'll call Kris. Kris was one of those people so bubbly, so glowing and so beautiful that next to her you felt dowdy even in your Sunday best. But she was so nice you couldn't even feel jealous of her! She seemed to do everything right: listen, befriend, encourage, pray, laugh and tell me how smart or clever I was. *If only I could be a friend like that*, I often thought.

The Example of Jesus

We may leave popularity contests behind us in high school, but we still like to be the one everyone gathers around at coffee break—that desire is as natural as wanting food or water or air. Perhaps even Jesus struggled with wanting to be liked. The Scriptures say He was tempted on all points like we are (Heb. 4:15). Could He have struggled with this most human desire, the desire to be popular? We know that one of the temptations dangled in front of Him was the possibility of becoming a popular Messiah, a wonder-working, bread-giving Savior (turning stones into bread—Matt. 4:3–4). And it surely must have been a heady experience to see throngs coming to Him from all over Galilee (Mark 3:7–8). Yet we know that Christ was without sin, and we can see that He kept His own popularity in perspective. He didn't seem to fear confronting the religious establishment (Mark 2:6—3:6) and being unpopular with the Pharisees and scribes. Moreover, among His closest followers He continually emphasized the kind of Messiah He *really* was, and that He must die (Mark 8:31). But even to the Garden of Gethsemane, Christ sweated out the desire to fulfill God's purposes another way (Mark 14:35–36).

To make popularity an idol is unacceptable for the Christian, but to want to be a likeable person is not. After all, only as we are approachable and open can we hope to be genuine in ministry.

To use Jesus as an example again: While Christ didn't

let popularity go to His head, He must have been a very charismatic person. When you consider, for instance, how quickly the disciples abandoned their occupations to follow Him (Mark 1:18, 20); when you grasp the density of the crowds that pressed around Him in an age with no mass communication (Mark 1:33, 45; 2:2–4); when you realize that His popularity developed in the short span of three years; when you catch His humor and wit, as in His humorous word pictures using camels (Matt. 19:24; 23:24), then you begin to sense the magnetism of His personality. From Christ's example we can thus say that there's nothing wrong with being likeable or wanting to be liked as long as it doesn't cause conceit.

What Do You Look For in a Friend?

So how can you be your best in friendship? Think of the people you like to be around. What makes them enjoyable?

"A good sense of humor" ranks first on many lists of "what I look for in a friend." Mothers are traditionally unpopular with their children and their children's friends during the pimples and Clearasil phase of life. But I remember the kids who came to our house frequently, saying, "We *like* your mom. She laughs at herself and is not afraid to act dumb with us."

Rob is a friend who loves to pun, and he's pretty good at it. On the surface he's a sober accountant, all business. But he unexpectedly livens up any card game or business meeting. A sense of humor is the lubricant that keeps any close living situation running smoothly.

On the other hand, a sense of humor has to be tempered with sensitivity to others. We all tire of the man who talks in overdrive, or the woman with a quadraphonic laugh. The sense of humor that helps us most is the one which laughs about the snake that got in the clothes dryer or that can smile back at an unexpected bill.

But certainly true friendliness goes far, far beyond an ability to laugh at life. An underlying key to being a likeable friend is being genuine. If a friend like Rob *only* communicates with jokes, how can we learn to like the real Rob?

Being genuine, refusing to deny even the most painful reality, can be a source of growth and learning for other people. I'll never forget the example of Challace McMillin, the head football coach at the university in our town. Challace advanced his team from Division III to Division I, but in doing so began to suffer several losing seasons. Injuries on the team were part of the reason.

Newspapers quipped that "the skids are already greased for McMillin's departure." Challace and his family are active members of our church, and at worship one Sunday morning many of us wondered quietly if the papers were right. Although I didn't know him well, I admired Challace and his family for coming to church on this difficult Sunday. It would have been much easier to stay home than to deal with emotions and questions up front.

For communion, we gathered in a large circle around the perimeter of the worship room. We sang the final hymn for the day, a parting song with words something like, "The time has come again for us to leave this place." The coach's teenage daughter began to cry visibly, and her mother offered a comforting arm.

Half the congregation was soon in tears. But it was a wonderful moment of solidarity, one I always recall when singing that song. And the best part was that even though Challace lost his coaching job, he made the gutsy decision to stick around and pursue a doctorate. In difficult times, Challace's example of vulnerability and openness—of not running away in crisis—always speaks to me. A friendship with a person like Challace is a relationship to treasure.

I again realized the value of risking openness during my recovery from the birth of our third child. It was a particularly trying time. Beforehand, I had worried how I would cope with *three* kids, and afterward I knew why I had worried. In addition to new-baby upheaval, we all had flu and fevers that hung on for three weeks. Furthermore, the baby was jaundiced and not nursing or sleeping well at night.

One morning when it seemed like I'd been up all night, the older girls were clamoring for breakfast and the baby was wanting to be fed, a knock came at the door. "Oh, no! There's no way I can hide these tears," I panicked.

It was my next-door neighbor. I couldn't let her in. I wanted to be cool, in control. I didn't want anybody to think I couldn't handle a situation.

But there she was, waiting, and I couldn't hide. As I let her in, I collapsed on her shoulder, explaining, "Oh, the baby's been up all night, and I'm exhausted!" It felt wonderful to let down that floodgate. She held me, and I remembered how my shoulder had served the same purpose for her not many years before when her husband died suddenly. I think it was because of this knowledge—that she had let me see *her* vulnerable side—that I felt free to be genuine with her. She helped me pull together breakfast for the girls before she dashed to work, and the rest of the day went better because of her.

Our Friends Help Us Grow

Being authentic and honest in communication generally helps people around us grow. While two people coping with the loss of a job each put up a front of indifference, that they're getting along okay and don't need anything, they remain alone in their frustration and disappointment. If one of them dares to say to the other, "Boy, it's really rotten, isn't it?", then encouragement and mutual help can begin.

But should we risk complete openness in front of *everyone*? Generally, when a casual acquaintance says, "How are you?" I can answer, "Fine." But a good friend wants to know about the *feelings* that underlie my daily work. So that's one place to begin risking honesty—telling how I'm really feeling to someone who sincerely wants to know. Most of us don't *want* to fake, or come off as fakes. And when I'm honest about how I'm feeling, my friend is freed to be honest too.

When my daughter Tanya was two, she still didn't talk very much. So when her older sister Michelle cried, Tanya simply went and patted Michelle gently on the head, looked worriedly into her face and fetched a tissue for the tears. Friendship means risking vulnerability; we can learn much from the example of children.

We wear masks because we feel the real "me" doesn't measure up—like when I was scared to host a slumber party. We don't think we're good enough. Unfortunately, many feel this about their spiritual lives as well.

John Catoir, a Catholic priest who produces radio and television programs, thinks large numbers of people are alienated from North American churches because they see the Church as an unforgiving place. They think that you have to be perfect to get in, stay in, and "make it to heaven." That's a most astonishing paradox, because the Church exists to be a *forgiving* people. Forgiving people are open people. If there's any place we should be able to be honest, it's within the Church.

But we're indoctrinated from youth about right and wrong religious habits. I had to catch myself when our four-year-old Michelle began making up her own bedtime prayers. She usually prayed very thoughtfully for needs she had seen during the day. But one night, she started praying for the characters on a TV show she had just watched. My impulse was to tell her what was wrong with her prayer, but I decided it wasn't a good moment for it. Talk about a good way to make her scared to pray in public! Later, in another context, I explained the difference between "real people" and "TV people."

In the same way, we can be ourselves before God—no

need for pretense because God knows and loves us just as we are. And that is the finest foundation of all for being a likeable person. Am I being honest with God? Do I believe in Jesus' death and resurrection in a personal way? If God loves me—and I believe that—I am free to be genuine with others, and a better friend in the process.

Specific Tips

1. Pick one trait (for example, a sense of humor) and concentrate on practicing it each day.

2. See if there's something humorous about your situation the instant you find yourself feeling depressed or upset by your circumstances.

3. Stop and ask yourself if you are truly being honest when you talk with your friends.

4. Relax. The people I know who are the most fun to be around don't constantly analyze every motive and action. They simply let themselves and others *be*!

MOTHER ALWAYS SAID, "PUT OTHERS FIRST"

CHAPTER TWO

Come May, we eagerly deposit long rows of corn kernels in the good earth. We bribe the girls to help us keep ahead of the weeds as spring rains bring lush growth. "Just think," we say. "If you help pull weeds now, you'll get to help eat corn-on-the-cob later on."

Along about July, the rains stop. We can usually harvest our first planting and then, despite watering, the last several plantings never develop. Without sufficient rain they never mature into the wonderful ears of corn we envisioned eating as we planted and weeded them.

It's the same way with people. Without sufficient nurture, we never develop into the wonderful human beings God had in mind when He created us.

Biblical Guidelines

Nurture means taking care of our own needs so that we have the personal resources to be genuine friends to others. But does this really apply to our relationships with others? How does it square with passages like Phil. 2:3–8?

> Do nothing out of selfish ambition or vain conceit, but

in humility consider others better than yourselves. Each of you should look not only to your own interests, but also to the interests of others. Your attitude should be the same as that of Christ Jesus: Who, being in very nature God, did not consider equality with God something to be grasped, but made himself nothing, taking the very nature of a servant being made in human likeness. And being found in appearance as a man, he humbled himself and became obedient to death—even death on a cross!

It's preached to us from our earliest days: "Let Johnny choose which piece of cake he wants." Surely, this unselfishness ranks high in any list of secrets of friendship. As Christians, we do believe in putting others first. "Be devoted to one another in kindred love, honor one another above yourselves" (Rom. 12:10, NIV) is another scripture that guides not only Christians but civilized society. Sharing, altruism and charity are right for any person.

This can mean things as practical as washing the dishes when your partner is exhausted, or giving a back rub for no reason at all. It can mean freeing your spouse to take a trip she's always wanted to take, even though you can't get away. Or it can mean taking your roommate's turn at cleaning the apartment when his workload is overwhelming.

This kind of give-and-take looks beyond the normal rules of who does what or what's expected. It's giving to someone out of love even when we don't feel like it or can't expect anything in return. It's sharing without worrying who got the biggest piece of pie.

How do we get to the place where we can *enjoy* putting others first—not because Mom and Dad told us it was the proper thing to do, but because it's what we *want* to do?

Personal Needs

We get to that place when our own needs are being met. As we learn to trust God to meet our needs—whatever they may be—we will then be able to act from an unselfish heart to love and serve others. It no longer is done out of drudgery, but rather from a willing heart. One young mother of three active boys put it this way: "I've come to see that my own need for recreation is as much of a need as food and rest. If I can't do something creative in my day, I'm miserable, and everyone else is too." She knits and bakes bread for recreation, although I'm not sure how she finds time.

Twice a year Ted and Connie travel home to visit his parents out-of-state. Everyone gets along fine. The kids look forward to the visit, Ted certainly does, and Connie likes being mothered once a year. But on the way home from one of these trips, Ted snapped at the kids and sulked. "I'm just tired. I'll be okay after some rest," he told himself. But why should a week of relaxation with no major responsibilities wear him out?

As he thought about it, he realized he was trying too hard to keep everyone content—by visiting all the relatives that were important to them, by keeping his wife happy and by taking the family places so they wouldn't get bored. And he was always spotting maintenance projects he wanted to do for his parents.

When Ted and Connie realized why he became so tired and irritable, they decided to take some vacations where they *didn't* visit family. At first that may sound selfish, but vacations weren't meant to make us more tired than staying home! A trip that leaves us physically, emotionally and mentally exhausted doesn't help anyone.

How do you get to know yourself well enough to discern these deep needs? Perhaps by trial-and-error. When life with two kids got too hectic, Wanda attempted to drop her part-time business of oil painting. But as she tried to quit, she found herself brooding and touchy. She knew they needed the money, and she also relished painting. She decided everyone would be happier if she made time for painting by delegating tasks or leaving less important chores undone.

Born to Serve

Yet putting others first goes deeper than seeing our own needs met. Let's go back to the corn. Ultimately, the purpose of the corn isn't to take its share of water just so it can sit there and grow plump, pretty ears. Ultimately, its purpose is to be *eaten*—sacrificed, used and enjoyed!

That's the goal for humans too. We take nourishment in order to prepare ourselves for service, for giving, to be used. It's okay to recognize that we have needs, but, like Christ, we in turn are to take on the nature of a servant (Phil. 2:7).

This means reorienting our whole lifestyle, not just resolving to "serve others" for five minutes. How difficult it is to accomplish that! It is a struggle common to all humans. The world caters to status, recognition, success, a name. Christians, however, are called to different priorities—not to "store up treasures for ourselves," but to "wash one another's feet."

On a practical level, many necessary chores occupy much of our day: The hedge needs trimming, the preschoolers beg to do a "project," and there's the 9-to-5 (or whatever) to put in. There's washing, cleaning, chauffeuring, each one consuming another chunk of time. To make room for personal reflection and resourcing and still have time for humble service after all the daily necessities of life might seem like an insurmountable task. I'm so thankful for the day-to-day witness of my parents' lives in this regard. Amidst all the activities that clamored for attention, they still found time to reach out and help many people.

Role Models

My parents often protest that I idealize them in my writings. But even though I realize they have a few shortcomings, their selfless giving had a definite influence on my life. Dad was a teenager during the Depression, the youngest child in a family of nine that lost their farm. After working in a mental hospital and a civilian public service camp as a conscientious objector during World War II, Dad went into debt to buy a small farm, but always continued his work of helping others.

Some of my earliest memories include frequent visits to a widow with little income who had two sons with severe mental disabilities. We brought groceries, helped with budgeting, cleaning, transportation, whatever was needed. His caring heart extended help to many other families throughout the years.

I remember going to other farms and playing in driveways as Dad solicited crops to send abroad for relief. One time Dad worked for months to organize the planting of an entire farm in one day. All the money earned from the crop was earmarked for "hungry people." Later, other farmers in other locations did the same. And I remember the valiant effort he and three partners made to provide jobs in the rural South by beginning a trailer manufacturing business. It floundered during a recession and they lost their life savings.

My mother's life has been one of dishpans, diapers, taking loads of corn to town, chasing hogs, and helping clean the homes of others (except for a brief stint as a secretary after business college). She was always there to help Dad in whatever he undertook. Her faithfulness in the many necessary details of everyday life has been a constant source of inspiration for me.

I suppose they would have liked to be rich, but I don't think that was ever an end in itself. Farming was a livelihood, service to others a way of life. Between the acts of reaching out, there was, of course, a whole host of mundane chores that were neither especially noble nor noteworthy— getting up in the morning, cultivating corn, gathering eggs and washing clothes. But all the while, Dad peppered us with statistics on hungry or needy people, and with comments like, "I hope at least one of my children goes into some kind of service."

Still, my parents were never "all work." In one pasture Dad dredged a place for a pond and built a small log cabin and cook-out grill. Mom's favorite family times were heading back to the cabin after a day of work for an evening of grilled hamburgers, fishing, swimming and listening to God speak through a chorus of bullfrogs!

If we want to become all that God meant us to be, we can look at the lives of other great servants to see how they combined service and "re-creation."

Specific Tips

1. Do I keep right on working when a neighbor comes over to talk, or do I sit down and give him or her my full attention? Do I take advantage of spur-of-the-moment opportunities to serve?

2. Am I giving a tithe (ten percent, either before or after taxes) of my income back to God? If not, could I move just one percent toward that goal, then next year another percent, and so on?

3. If I catch myself wishing for something I don't need, can I use that as a trigger to stop and thank God for one blessing I already have?

4. Could I give up one family meal at a restaurant ($15 or more) each month and send the money to hunger relief?

5. Teachers expect three hours of preparation for every hour spent in the classroom. Is it possible to develop a personal rule of thumb such as one hour of personal time/meditation for every three hours of service/outreach activity?

I ALWAYS HATED TO SHARE A PIECE OF GUM

CHAPTER THREE

I have a confession to make to all of my childhood friends: I was (maybe still am) a louse. My friends generously shared whatever gum or candy they had, but I quietly unwrapped any gum stashed in *my* purse so I wouldn't have to share it. Shame and double shame, but I suspect I wasn't alone.

My friend George, however, was *never* like that. He once told me, "I'm such a sucker, Melodie. I can't hang on to money. If a friend needs shoes and he doesn't have money for them, I'll give him the money I have."

I knew George wasn't bragging. He was complaining! Flashing a ten-yard smile and never worried about the money he spent on his friends, he had the kind of charisma that attracted men and women alike. Once when a guy passed out from too much alcohol and everyone else was snickering, George tenderly carried him to a bed and tucked covers around him. As the good Samaritan, George told the stupored fellow he'd check on him in the morning. I felt like the priest or Levite, too good to get involved with someone different from me, especially one with a drinking problem.

What made George the kind of friend I'd like to be?

Huge doses of unselfishness. I can't imagine him ever, *ever*—not even in his childhood—secretly hoarding a piece of gum so he wouldn't have to share. While I worried about associating with a drunk person for fear of being wrongly labeled, George figured that showing love came before making a good impression. To be fair, if George had a fault it was that he naturally assumed others were as free with their money and possessions as he was. He thought nothing of borrowing five dollars and forgetting to pay it back.

George was free with his possessions, a trait I see as being biblical and integral to friendship, but very, very difficult. As Jesus succinctly put it, "It is easier for a camel to go through the eye of a needle than for a rich man to enter the kingdom of God" (Mark 10:25, NIV).

How Much Should We Share?

Like the disciples, we're left wondering—*how rich is rich?* Do I have to take vows of poverty to make it into the kingdom of God? Exactly how free of possessions must I be?

The good news is that Jesus follows up by saying, "With humans this is impossible, but all things are possible with God" (Mark 10:27, paraphrased). If we understand that "the kingdom of God" has already begun—with Jesus' life, death and resurrection on earth—and that the Christian is living as a citizen of two kingdoms—an earthly kingdom (nation) and a spiritual kingdom—then we can understand why it is extremely difficult for a rich person to become a Christian. When we begin to see what Christ calls us to in a life of discipleship—for instance, to be with the poor and needy—then we see 101 places to use our money and we must respond. As true citizens of the kingdom of God, we will *want* to give away so much money that we won't be "rich."

To be the kind of person God wants us to be, we must

develop this freedom from possessions. This is one secret of friendship.

I do think that there will always be some who are wealthier than others, and that people who have more money can do *much* good by investing wisely and then giving generously to numerous causes, as so many wealthy Christians do. But Jesus calls amassing vast fortunes for the sake of having vast fortunes an impossibility for the Christian.

The idea that maybe we don't deserve to have more and more goes against the grain of North American society. One of the commercials I dislike most says, "It costs a little more, but *I'm* worth it." Our whole Western view of the world says that bigger is better, the latest model will do more than the last, that more is worth it—and furthermore, that I deserve it!

Surely, I tell myself, I'm immune to this push to acquire more and more. I won't be sucked in by shallow promises of a more glamorous life. Then I look at my closet—simple by many standards. Yet compared to my counterparts in India or Southeast Asia or Central America, it is abundant. Someone more blunt might call it greedy.

In the 1970s professor John Taylor's *Enough Is Enough*[1] was somewhat of an underground Christian classic in England. Taylor urged people to liberate themselves from the tyranny of always planning the next purchase.

But isn't it a farce to try to live a simpler life? Being able to ask myself that question is in itself a luxury—living a simpler life can only be a middle-income person's concern. It's one thing for some well-paid professor to decide that "enough is enough" and urge people to get by on less. It's quite another to tell that to someone who's owned only one pair of shoes at a time for most of his life.

It is reasonable to want a little more, to see our economy

---

[1] John V. Taylor, *Enough Is Enough* (Minneapolis: Augsburg Publishing House, 1977).

grow, and to have life become more convenient. And businesses need to operate with a profit margin. So I'm not anti-progress or anti-business. But I do think all of us would be happier, live freer, if we could somehow get this monkey of greed off our backs.

For instance, we could share rather than purchase more things. Tomorrow count the passengers in the cars you pass on your way to or from work. Most have just one passenger! Or notice the homes on the block with a grass trimmer—and I'm not even talking about lawn mowers here! I know several friends who live in separate homes but pool their garden tools and space. It takes cooperation and planning, and in their case even a special checking account. I admire the interdependence this sharing requires.

Another inroad for this attitude is our desire to want everything too fast. Sweepstakes and lotteries make us dream of becoming millionaires overnight. Young couples rush to buy all the things their parents had, forgetting it took their parents years to acquire them.

I'm reminded of the old tale where a fisherman catches a flounder that turns out to be a prince who is able to grant any wish. When the fisherman tells his wife about his eventful catch, she inquires, "Well, husband, what did you wish for?"

"Nothing," the fisherman answers. "Aren't we happy here?"

"Happy? Here in this horrible hut? Ha! I should say not! Ask for a cottage!"

The fisherman sees that this is reasonable and goes off to ask his fish. But the cottage isn't enough. Human being that she is, the wife next dares to demand a castle with a golden throne. After that only the universe will do—she wants to rule the moon and sun. But the fish decides that this is too much, that now they shall have nothing. And so the fisherman and his wife are back in the dark, dirty hut where they began. Even if we bristle at the stereotype of the wife being the one who begs for more, the fairy tale preaches a simple but appropriate moral.

Satisfaction Guaranteed

I'm encouraged when I see people consciously trying to be satisfied with what they have, for example, with their housing. Like the fisherman's wife, we are concerned about our homes. Buying or renting a place to live will probably be the greatest expense most of us will encounter over the course of a lifetime. Add utilities, furnishings and repairs, and our homes end up demanding most of our income and energy. If we want to try to be more satisfied with what we have and more giving in our relationships, being more satisfied with our homes would be a good place to start.

In Doris Janzen Longacre's *Living More With Less*, a former missionary to India describes how on their return to North America a hostess asked if they had a nice house in India. Herta remembered cockroaches, mice and rats coming up drains, torn screens and broken windowpanes, bats flying through the dining room during mealtime, and a toilet that needed an instruction booklet to operate. Before she had a chance to answer her hostess's question, her eight-year-old son responded enthusiastically, "Oh, yes! We had a real nice house in Calcutta."

What made her son call such a broken down house nice? The life there, of course. Herta reflected some more and remembered the games they played, the reading, talking, listening, learning and singing. They had entertained many guests. In short, it was a nice house because it was home.[2]

A home with adequate space does seem basic to happiness. It gives us refuge, a place to revitalize energies for relating to others. Everyone needs a home, but perhaps we need to remodel our ideas of our dream house.

---

[2]Doris Janzen Longacre, *Living More With Less* (Scottsdale, Penn.: Herald Press, 1980), p. 123.

Wanting bigger and better homes isn't all that stands in the way of being a friend. One pundit said that the difference between Patrick Henry and the average person today is that while Patrick Henry said, "Give me liberty or give me death," the typical person today just says, "Gimme."

Are most people really that selfish? Well, yes—and no. Mother Teresa has devoted her life to helping the poorest of the poor. You might counter that she hardly qualifies as typical, but in the beginning she was an average woman who never dreamed of winning the Nobel prize for her work. Others demonstrate that average people can be servants. A doctor from Maryland gave up a thriving practice and a sizable salary to work at a health clinic in Washington, D.C. Another woman left her job in order to visit regularly with women in prison. Volunteers in Texas refurbish homes at no cost to the residents, teaching them carpentry skills at the same time.

Clearly, there are many examples of average people who *aren't* out for all they can get. Yet greed persists. "Avarice" was the old-fashioned term, and it was called one of the seven deadly sins. "Thou shalt not covet" is the Old Testament commandment.

Downsizing

How can we tame the monster of greed within us? We begin by paring down our expectations of what is enough. Ron and Mim both hold jobs, and for many years they have gotten by with one car. Sometimes the hassle of coordinating the use of the car seems to take more energy and emotional expense than just buying a second car. But it is one way they have decided that enough is enough.

I hate the twelve-year-old gold drapes in the living room of our house. Every once in a while I browse through a catalog and imagine how much better our house would look with something fresher. But I have trouble justifying the expense when I know many people would be glad to have a *house* as big as our living room.

It's not wrong to buy a second car or new drapes, but these are ways people say, "We have more than enough. This is one way I'll make do." Staying away from car dealerships and not looking at catalogs can be two practical ways of taming the greed within us!

Freedom From the Obsession of Greed

Aren't these just superficial gestures? What lasting benefit comes from trying to get by with what we have, rather than always looking for more? What does this have to do with the secret of friendship?

Beliefs and philosophies aren't much good until we put them into practice. First, as we make the small gesture of being content with one car, we give meaning to our beliefs. We build small steps to larger gestures.

The second reason for trying to be satisfied with what we have is that it is tremendously freeing. When we're tempted to think that our money never goes far enough or that things will surely get better after the next raise, we would be wise to try to be happy if we have food and work and faith in God (Eccles. 3:22).

Ted had few possessions, even as a child. Raised in a foster home, he lost touch with his parents and other family members. As a youth he got into trouble with the law, and spent a third of his life in prison. But there his life started turning around.

A group from our church visited his prison each week, and when Ted finally made parole, this group became his family, support and help. He stayed clean, and after five years his voting rights were restored. Even then he didn't have an easy time. He had some trouble managing his money, but he held a job and kept a small apartment.

But that wasn't all. In the last years of his life, besides

visiting others in prison, Ted and his friends from church started working with youths who seemed headed for trouble. They took these kids to a state correctional institution to talk with the inmates. Ted was determined to help others not make the mistakes he had made.

When Ted died several years ago, no one knew his age for sure. There was no family to notify. No reason to spend money on a casket, burial plot and funeral. So after worship one Sunday morning, the children gathered wildflowers and the church family took his ashes and buried them beneath a tree beside the church. In the afternoon, there was a memorial service celebrating Ted's life and work.

Ted had little money. His greatest joy was his friendship with the youths. He was happy to be a free man.

The best friend is one not overly concerned with getting ahead—nor so concerned with a simplified lifestyle that he or she neglects relationships! The Bible speaks of being "steadfast in purpose" (Acts 11:23, RSV). As we focus our energies on living God's way, we can weed out the extras that crowd our lives, and make room for fellowship and friendship with others.

Specific Tips:

1. If sharing is difficult for you, look for ways to give of yourself or possessions at least once this week.

2. Make a list of "Things I Don't Need" and a list of "Things I Need." (I'm thinking of both tangible and intangible items here.) Pick two items on the second list and think about ways you can meet your needs. For example, if I need "friends" and "family," what are two ways I can give priority to those needs?

3. Page through a catalog—by yourself or with a child—and choose the "Dumbest/Least Necessary Items" on each page.

4. As a family, sit down with a year's calendar and plan "giving opportunities" for each month. These can be simple (visit Aunt Sara) to more costly (helping out someone with financial needs).

ACTING LIKE YOU STILL HAD BRACES ON YOUR TEETH

CHAPTER FOUR

I suppose one of the first things I think of when considering secrets of friendship is how far an engaging, sincere smile goes in beginning and continuing a relationship. Look how far Jimmy Carter's smile took him! How easily some flash their pearly whites. Most of the rest of us act like we still had braces on our teeth.

Now, I've never worn braces, and that's why I prefer to smile with my mouth closed. My teeth aren't crooked, but a friendly gap between my two front teeth sometimes makes me camera-shy.

A college friend I'll call Sue had a model's smile. It was probably obtained from her orthodontist. With blue eyes and blond hair to the middle of her back, she was definitely a heart-stopper.

And her smile was genuine. Trusting in others almost to a fault, she attracted crowds of both guys and female friends. She was so adept at spreading out the attention she received that it took months before I realized guys talked to us because of *her*, not because of the rest of us!

That radiance doesn't come from using the right toothpaste. Sue's Christian walk hadn't been free of ups and downs—which is perhaps why the joy she exuded was so attractive. At one point, she became sexually involved with a non-Christian man. She felt terribly guilty, and struggled for months over ending the relationship. Her own parents weren't Christians either, which caused her more pain. Her struggle back to victory was a painful one, but her experiences made her especially sensitive to others' hurts. Knowing firsthand how easy it is to sin made her unwilling to ever cast the first stone.

The Source of Joy

What is the source of Christian joy? It springs from a right relationship with God through Jesus' love and sacrifice. John 15:10–11 says it well: "If you obey my commands, you will remain in my love, just as I have obeyed my Father's commands and remain in his love. I have told you this so that my joy may be in you and that *your joy may be complete*" (NIV).

Anyone—Christian or not—can know deep joy. But "joy that is complete" comes through Christ. Even then, as a favorite hymn says, ". . . All our joy is touched with pain, that shadows fall on brightest hours, that thorns remain—so that earth's bliss may be our guide and not our chain."[1]

Not everyone who jots "Christian" on the dotted line marked "religion" smiles from never-ending joy and satisfaction. So how do we work at becoming someone whose smile displays deep inner contentment? Meaningful work, family, friends and faith are ready answers to that question. But let's look beyond those at some other pillars that undergird personal joy.

Roots

First, we need a sense of rootedness, of security. For a long time I didn't want to settle down. For nine years I lived

---

[1] "My God, I Thank Thee," Adelaide Proctor, *The Mennonite Hymnal* (Scottdale, Penn.: Herald Press, 1969), p. 267. Public domain.

in a different place every year: Indiana, Florida, Kentucky, Virginia in a dormitory, then a household of fourteen people, Spain, back to Virginia to an apartment, a different apartment, a trailer. Then, finally, a year after I married we bought a country home—a little white house with a white picket fence and two maples in the front yard!

In the fall, I planted tulip bulbs, and felt wonderful that we'd be there the following spring to enjoy them. But another part of me still longed to wander the streets of strange cities and explore the unknown. The births of our children helped me push roots further into our little acre of ground, but I continued to envy friends who lived in Yugoslavia, Italy and Africa.

One evening my husband and I were talking about moving to a different house. We soon discovered the kids' view of the matter! "But this is our *home!*" they protested. "We don't want to get another home." To the children, moving sounded as foreign and undesirable as getting a different set of parents.

Soon after, I read one researcher's opinion on why teenage suicide has climbed forty-four percent since 1970. This researcher felt that frequent moves and lack of extended family partially explained rampant teen suicides. One teen in Houston hung himself in a tree and left this note: "This is the only thing around here that has any roots."[2]

I began to realize that staying put wasn't so awful. We're giving our children something just as valuable as adventure and new experiences: the gift of rootedness.

Let me hasten to add that I don't believe for a minute that all families who move frequently lack roots. There is a quality of family life that brings security in spite of the moves a family has to make.

Then what contributes to a stable family life, one in which every child feels he or she belongs? Roots don't come

---

[2]*Sources and Resources*, December 1984, p. 1.

from living in the same house all your life. They extend between the family members themselves and between people in the community, whether related by blood or not.

If we grew up without this feeling of belonging to other people, we can develop it by finding a small group of people at church. Over time, a sense of family grows where we can share our lives and thoughts. Feeling rooted contributes to genuine joy—and fills out our smiles.

Using Gifts

Secondly, inner joy comes from knowing our talents and using them. Even after several cataract surgeries my ninety-one-year-old grandmother still occasionally works as a seamstress doing intricate alterations. Grandma's career may have not been the most glamorous in the world, but she has always been an embodiment of true humility. So I was pleased when she wrote once of sewing as her "talent." Feeling good about personal skills and recognizing them as a gift from God is bound to bring self-esteem and happiness.

Perhaps you honestly think you're not good at anything. Make a list of things you *enjoy* doing. Even if you think you're not very good at something, write it down. Now *make* something a talent. Pick one item off your list and start working on it at least once a week. Few people come loaded with natural talents. Most develop them. Ask God to guide your focus, and get involved in an organization or group of people who practice the same hobby or skill for professional feedback and inspiration.

Attitude

A third way to know inner joy is to get to the place where you can thank God even for routine days. We get up, have breakfast, go to work at home or away, have lunch, occupy ourselves till evening and then relax a few hours until bedtime. Sometimes it gets old, but the key to living fully is learning to enjoy these ordinary days.

Ordinary days are the ones when you're *not* confined to a hospital bed or facing the trauma of divorce or death of a loved one. If ordinary days slide by, one just like the other, we should celebrate that we're healthy, alert and happy instead of complaining about the sameness.

Tragedy suspends routine. Days blend into weeks while life revolves around the hospital, doctors' reports and visiting hours. The cycle of breakfast, lunch and supper is haphazard, not so important. People who've been sent to jail or lost a child or had a spouse suddenly walk out find their world turned upside-down. So when we have *ordinary* days we should be grateful. A grateful heart tends to unlock the fountains of joy.

But we can do more than that. All around us are people who *aren't* having ordinary days! A friend whose husband died suddenly described her plight: "Everyone else's life seemed to go on as usual, while mine had changed forever. I wanted to scream at the people driving to their jobs, 'How can you go about business as usual? Something has happened to me!' "

Life does go on, but those in traumatic situations generally appreciate those who stop their worlds for a few hours or days to grieve, to offer assistance, to upset normal schedules to be with them in their crisis. "Do for others as you would want them to do for you," Jesus said (Matt. 7:12). Remember that—in ordinary or extraordinary days.

Specific Tips

1. Every day this week smile big at your spouse or roommate upon arriving home. See how long it takes for him or her to ask, "What's up?"

2. Bestow a genuine smile upon a stranger each day. What reactions do you get?

3. What gives you joy? Prepare your own list of personal keys to joy. Mine were rootedness, having talents, ordinary days.

4. Sing—if you know the tune—or pray Adelaide Proctor's lovely hymn:

"MY GOD, I THANK THEE!"

My God, I thank Thee, who hast made the earth so
    bright,
So full of splendor and of joy, beauty and light,
So many glorious things are here, noble and right.
I thank Thee, too, that Thou hast made joy to abound,
So many gentle thoughts and deeds circling us round;
That in the darkest spot of earth some love is found.
I thank Thee more that all our joy is touched with pain;
That shadows fall on brightest hours, that thorns
    remain,
So that earth's bliss may be our guide, and not our chain.
I thank Thee, Lord, that Thou hast kept the best in
    store;
We have enough, yet not too much to long for more,
A yearning for a deeper peace not known before.

LIKEABLE PEOPLE DON'T MIND THE DUST

CHAPTER FIVE

A cross-stitched sign hangs right inside the front door of Polly's house, in a place where you normally don't see it until you're ready to leave. I would like to get my own copy: "A well-kept house is the sign of a misspent life." I've liked Polly's motto even more since she told me the story behind the sign. She has a relative whose house always looks lovely, and Polly was inclined to apologize profusely for her house whenever this relative came to visit. One day the relative brought Polly the little cross-stitched motto.

Before you assume Polly's house is a pigpen, you should know that it is not. The living room is a picture of hominess, beauty and good taste. Well-used books and a lifetime of mementoes line one wall. Another section is a montage of family pictures. Still another features lithographs, art from friends, signed posters. A low table in the middle may sport a huge bouquet of fresh lilacs or nothing but bread and grape juice for a small-group communion service.

She, her husband and another couple have taken turns almost every week this past year hosting every person and family in our small congregation for a no-strings-attached scrumptious meal. We've teased them that they could easily open a diner; Polly prefers to keep it a labor of love.

If my house were perfectly kept, would I take offense at Polly's sign? Probably not. People whose houses look to me in perfect order almost always say, "You'll have to excuse the mess." So they probably wouldn't think that Polly's sign implied they were misspending their lives. And I don't think Polly is targeting anyone else's house. *If* things seem chaotic or out of order here, she seems to be saying, "It's because I have other priorities."

Polly is a person to whom I take a special prayer request, knowing that she'll really pray and care about the outcome. If I ever get around to inviting her back for a meal, I won't worry too much about dust and disorder. She reminds me that one secret of friendship is the ability not to worry about attaining some worldly superwoman status.

Too Good to Be True

The media are filled with heroes and super-heros. Some are the cartoon kind—Superman, She-Ra, He-Man. Then there are "real-life" wonder people: super-working mother, perfect TV father. Remember the "Incredible Hulk," the half monster/half man a few years back on TV? When my daughter Michelle was three, she mistakenly called him the "*Cred*ible Hulk." Too often we make the mistake of believing that "real-life" wonder people are credible too—that they represent attainable goals.

When we admire people who seem to be incredibly good at everything they do, we seldom realize there may also be things they aren't doing. For instance, most employed mothers who are realistic don't claim they can manage everything. One mom admits she has absolutely no social life; another claims her house is a disaster area; another says she has given up all volunteer work and club involvements. So when you feel inadequate in comparison to people who seem much more accomplished and successful, remember that they probably have areas of life where they feel like failures, too.

Occasionally, I feel really burnt out—beleaguered by too many things and too little time. So I try to cheer myself up by reminding myself, "You did four good things today: You washed the diapers, entertained the guests you'd been wanting to invite for a long time, made a tasty supper, and kept your kids happy."

But instead of feeling cheered, I worry about the mess in the basement that sneers at me everytime I descend the stairs. The spider webs and fingerprints and everlasting clutter do me in. The undone, the half-done, the never-done dog me, making me tired and unsatisfied with the few things I do manage to get done.

This much is clear: It's hard to be pleasant when we feel swamped! And no one likes to be around a grouch. What can we do when we feel this way?

Concentrate on Accomplishments

First, force yourself to concentrate *only* on the good things you've accomplished. There will always be more to do. The most unsatisfied people are the ones who can never enjoy a few moments of completion, who never take a break or reward themselves for sticking to a difficult task.

Plan Variety

One busy teacher divides her time into blocks for variety: when home on a Saturday she grades papers for two hours, works outside for two hours and then cleans for two hours. (With no children, she has fewer interruptions!)

Start Small

Another way to get rid of the too-much-to-do-in-too-little-time feeling is to tackle just part of a nasty job—a *corner* of that messy basement, for instance. It's amazing how much clutter can be straightened in fifteen minutes. Or if it's a stack of correspondence on your desk at work that's bothering you, try to type three letters instead of the whole pile. Getting started is half the work in almost anything. Then allow yourself to feel good about that wonderful-looking corner or those three neat letters.

Delegate Work

With good intentions we sometimes do things that others could or should be doing. By erroneously thinking we have to do everything or solve everyone's problem, we wear ourselves out. It's not helpful to children, for example, for you to do all their work for them. They can straighten their rooms and put away their toys, and do errands and odd jobs. By delegating various jobs, you not only alleviate yourself from an overload, but you help others learn to be responsible.

Sort Your Worries

One day several years ago I was feeling particularly depressed. I decided to write down everything bothering me at the moment—lack of money, not having time to clean house, Michelle's potty training, my husband's job, the baby's slowness in doing things, a pulled muscle, needing to work outside the home, not having more friendships and Michelle's eating habits.

Then I went back and labeled each item with an "A," "B" or "C." A's were things I knew I could work to try to change. B's were things I realistically couldn't change. And C's were things that in time would change without much effort if I had patience. I ended up with only two A's— things I wanted to try to change, like improving friendships. I tried to ignore the things I couldn't change anyway, and now, as I look back years later, the C's—things like potty training and the baby's slowness—really did take care of themselves.

If you're burdened by a number of things, it might help to list and letter them as I did. Keep the list, and look back in three months to see if there's been progress. When we feel more on top of our worries and busy schedules, we're freer to have time for friends.

Sometimes the load we feel is hard to put a finger on. Maybe we're worried about a daughter's studies, a parent's illness or the nuclear threat. Perhaps we're pressed by guilt for an old wrong or by an over-arching feeling of failure.

Life doesn't come with guarantees of happiness or freedom from overload. In fact, if anything can be guaranteed it's that each person will have his or her share of problems. We joke about how soap operas unrealistically pile problem upon problem, while the lives of ordinary people are as mixed up and stressful as those on TV. "If someone put my family's story in a novel," says a friend, "critics would call it unrealistic!" Death, spouse abuse, drugs, unwanted pregnancies, divorce, a runaway child—these happen in the best of families.

So what happens to you isn't as important as how you handle it. We can *make* happiness a habit. There *are* some ingredients essential to happiness: loving at least one other human being, having a few responsibilities that make us feel needed, and being dedicated to a larger purpose or worthwhile cause. When you pursue happiness as an object in itself, it is difficult to catch. It always seems to elude you.

Perhaps you're saying, "I really don't feel overwhelmed right now. This chapter just isn't for me." I do know people like that—people who at least say they don't have any major problems. If that's the case, Scripture encourages us to "bear one another's burdens" (Gal. 6:2). Lift the load for someone else. Be available to listen or to help when someone confides in you.

When too many demands press us, we can remember

that each season of life brings its own joys and its own burdens. I was envying the beautiful, weed-free garden of my husband's aunt and uncle. "If only I didn't have toddlers underfoot all the time, our garden could look like that too," I lamented. Then I noticed again Aunt Edith's limp, and listened to her describe her pain. I realized that by the time I get to the place in life where I can have a perfect garden, I might not have the physical strength or ability to handle it. And the years between now and then will probably be too busy to ever get caught up with things.

But whatever the season of life, we can make ourselves happier by accepting the accompanying limitations. Yet at the same time, we can also learn to rid ourselves of unnecessary burdens—the unrealistic goal, for example, of having a perfect garden while taking care of toddlers.

Living free is a state of mind, an attitude we can learn— and is one more secret of friendship.

Specific Tips:

1. Decide on an appropriate motto for your house or kitchen. Post it for all to see if you wish.

2. Write down the things you're concerned about. Label them:

A. Things I can change

B. Things I can't change

C. Things that will take care of themselves.

Put a reminder on your calendar to check your list six months from now.

3. Read Eccles. 3:1–8. If you enjoy writing, try an appropriate paraphrase describing your life right now. Or do an interpretive dance or make an object of art.

4. Fill in the blanks.

My most pressing concern right now is: _____.

If I don't/can't do anything, this will happen: _____.

Therefore, I will do this _____.

THREE OF THE BEST-KEPT SECRETS FOR BEING MORE LIKEABLE

CHAPTER SIX

Adam throws a tantrum in the supermarket. His father tells a disapproving onlooker, "He's really tired tonight. He didn't have his nap today."

We all sometimes act like grouchy toddlers when we don't get our normal amount of sleep. Research shows how lack of sleep can drastically change personality—like that horrible morning I mentioned in chapter one. Nights of no sleep had reduced me to classic post-partum depression. (So why can't I be more patient when my own preschoolers unravel from lack of sleep?)

Secret #1: Get Enough Sleep

When I think of ways to be my best in relationships, I place high priority on getting enough rest. Sleep is the great restorer, a sometimes overlooked source of strength and vivaciousness.

One executive thinks sleep is so important that he doesn't mind people falling asleep while he's talking in a meeting. "If you need to sleep, go ahead and get it out of the way. Then you can be more alert for the rest of the meeting," he tells his employees. Not all executives are so understanding, but it's amazing what sneaking even a five-minute catnap will do to restore productivity.

Of course, if you sleep through every meeting you might need to find other solutions. First, go to bed earlier. Second, be aware of your natural body rhythms—whether you're a morning person or a night person.

Third, you may need exercise. I alternate between periods of regular exercise and months of laziness. I always feel better and more peppy (especially in the morning) when I make myself exercise, but often I don't have time or it's too boring. But scientists have documented that strenuous workouts of at least twenty minutes three times a week actually give us a chemical lift.

Fourth, your diet may not be providing the right vitamins and minerals. These deficiencies can also cause chronic tiredness. I and many women suffer from iron-poor blood— Ted Macks' old commercials for Geritol weren't just hype! While megadoses of vitamins aren't necessary—and may even be harmful—many doctors do advise taking iron or calcium supplements for special needs.

Secret #2: Spend Time Alone

The real secret of being a likeable person, however, lies far deeper than sleep or health. When we give of ourselves all day long, we must be replenished. "Every person, especially every woman," writes Anne Morrow Lindbergh, "should be alone sometime during the year, some part of each week, and each day."[1]

Lindbergh admits that these words from her classic book *Gift From the Sea* sound revolutionary and impossible to achieve. But, she says, "Certain springs are tapped only

---

[1]Anne Morrow Lindbergh, *Gift From the Sea* (New York: Vintage Books, 1975), p. 48.

when we are alone."[2] If we really believe that time alone is a fundamental need, we will arrange for that even if we can't hire a babysitter or escape from a factory assembly line.

But finding time for yourself is a major obstacle. You plan for a quiet time early in the morning and, of course, that's the morning the kids wake earlier than usual. You promise it to yourself at the end of the day, but by that time you just want to curl up and go to bed. In spite of the difficulties, being committed to finding time for yourself can help you find it, perhaps unexpectedly. Having a regular place to be alone or having a specific book or meditation to use can help you be serious about taking time out.

For those who enjoy writing, keeping a journal gives some reflection time. You don't have to slavishly write in it every day or even every week, but periodically write down feelings, significant milestones and little conversations. Jogging is physically and emotionally renewing for many. Perhaps you can claim Sunday morning in church as your special time.

Lindbergh says society understands neither man's nor woman's need to be alone. She writes, "If one sets aside time for a business appointment, a trip to the hairdresser, a social engagement, or a shopping expedition, that time is accepted as inviolable. But if one says, 'I cannot come because that is my hour to be alone,' one is considered rude, egotistical, or strange.

"What a commentary on our civilization," Lindbergh goes on, "when being alone is considered suspect; when one has to apologize for it, make excuses, hide the fact that one practices it, like a secret vice!"[3]

I'm learning not to apologize for the need to be alone. And I encourage others to do the same! It can make the difference between normal, happy tiredness and burn-out.

---

[2]Ibid., p. 50.
[3]Ibid.

Secret #3: Reach Out to Others

Perhaps you're on the other end of things—you have too much time alone. Somehow the long-ago days filled with toddlers and toys look inviting now. If this is your situation, then the key to being more likeable is just the opposite. Rather than drawing back and taking time to be alone, find activities that help you reach out. It's surprising how much better we feel and how much more likeable we are when we have work to take our minds off ourselves. If we've taken time through the years to cultivate plenty of interests, we'll be happier when loneliness strikes.

We become more attractive to others by spreading our love around. First Corinthians 13 says that if we say we love others but don't show it by our actions, then our words are meaningless.

The possibilities for reaching out are limited only by your health and imagination. You can volunteer at a hospital or nursing home, or be an advocate friend for people with physical or mental disabilities. In our medium-sized community, I know of programs where volunteers serve as tutors, literacy instructors, Big Brothers/Sisters, hospice workers and respite care-givers for those keeping elderly or ill persons in their homes. Some volunteers help settle disputes out of court through a community mediation program. Others work at senior citizen centers, write to people in prison or help at nursery schools and day-care centers. Suicide prevention hotlines, spouse abuse programs and foster parent and grandparent programs also need people with giving hearts.

You don't have to work through an organized program at all. Take time to love the kid who hangs around your house after school because no one is home at his house. A teenager may need time with you—for teens, zits loom larger than life, teachers just don't understand and heartbreaks are hard to survive. The nosey person next door might just need a friend, and new neighbors always need our welcoming gestures. In short, there is little excuse for not being as busy as you want to be and as health permits.

What good does all this work do? "Love never fails," says the familiar Bible verse in 1 Cor. 13:8. Still, in spite of all our best efforts, love sometimes *seems* to fail. Every one of the volunteer outlets I've listed is fraught with possibilities for failure: Loving, dedicated volunteers sometimes feel used and taken for granted. Or a teenage girl you befriend to bring a "good influence" winds up pregnant and unmarried anyway. Runaways don't automatically come home, estranged husbands and wives sometimes remain distant, and your neighborhood might not become the caring community you want it to be. Our world is a place full of human, failing people. At those times, it is faith in God that keeps us functioning, loving, even when answers don't come.

Cancer will continue, drunk drivers will still kill, floods will rise again. Sometimes love only makes a difference inside *you*, but that can be the difference between giving up and keeping on.

It's helpful to reflect how being hurt by unreturned love can help us to mature. Perhaps we judge character more realistically. We learn to take things slower. We decide to let children make their own mistakes.

Loving others isn't easy, but if we take time for ourselves and learn to love *ourselves*, we will have more energy and resources for extending love and friendship to others. As we take time to be in His presence, we will find ourselves replenished and able to go out and extend that love to others.

Each of us lives somewhere on a continuum of busyness. For those overwhelmed by kids, jobs and responsibilities, the secret of being more likeable may well be more time alone—for growth, spiritual renewal, even for sleep. For those bored by loneliness and too little to do, new work and reaching out may uncap a fresh wellspring of joy.

Specific Tips:

1. Are you tired or grouchy? See if an occasional nap or a multivitamin (with iron) makes a difference in how you feel.

2. Pick two of ideas under Secret #3, put deadlines on them, and ask someone to check with you on how it's going.

3. Experiment with a *regular* quiet time. Don't try to spend large blocks of time at first. It is better to start with ten or fifteen minutes. Let desire increase it, not guilt or obligation.

4. If you're not already too busy, consider finding one volunteer activity to give you new resources for being a more interesting person.

A LITTLE CHILD SHALL LEAD THEM

CHAPTER SEVEN

W ho would slosh through pelting rain and inches of mud to plunk down seven dollars a head—and then sit shivering in a giant old circus tent? "This is crazy," I told myself. "I can't believe I'm paying a buck for a cold hot dog and another buck for a warm soft drink, just to sit here with Gwen and our kids because this is the only day the circus will be in town."

I spied an acquaintance as we stood in line for balloons at intermission and yelled, "I see we're not the only crazy ones here!" Larry grinned back, "Yeah, so far I've only spent $23!" We both shook our heads at the extravagance, and I thought again of the nerve of a vendor trying to shovel off $2 snow cones on a freezing day. The clowns in *this* circus weren't all in the show rings!

Yet, childhood and circuses are practically synonymous to me, even though as a child I never went to even one. Maybe it was because I'd never been to one as a child that I made this a high priority. Our kids had been looking forward to their first circus for weeks, and to cancel at the last minute because of rain would have been a betrayal tantamount to canceling Christmas.

We shared popcorn as I pointed out parading poodles and swash-buckling lion-tamers so the four-year-old wouldn't miss anything. By the time the tumblers from Morocco sprang around the center circle, I was clapping as loudly as the children, begging with the crowd for more.

But the sight that warmed me more than any act in the ring was seventeen wheelchairs lined up in front of the grandstands. In the wheelchairs sat folks from a nearby nursing home watching the circus from behind rain hats, their eyes as bright as any kid's.

I thought of a lot of people who would have had a dozen reasonable excuses for not going out on such a day. Suddenly, I knew that even rain and rip-off prices were a small price to pay for the warmth of the small hands clutched in mine as we hurried laughing and muddy to the car.

If I'm still healthy at seventy-five or eighty, I hope I'll still have enough child in me to wheel it to the circus even through a chilling spring rain.

Am I all wet to think that a childlike sense of wonder is a worthwhile trait? Aren't some of the most likeable people you know those who still have a bit of a kid in them? Not childishness, of course, but a heart that doesn't prejudge others and a willingness to let down their hair from time to time?

The Gift of Wonder

The mother of one foster child was perplexed. "He doesn't *wonder* about things like most kids do. We take him someplace new or on a drive to the mountains, and he doesn't ask any questions." Most parents will agree that children are blessed with a sometimes-exasperating gift of wonder. "Why did God make the clouds so high?" When I admitted that I didn't know, Michelle was ready with her own answer: "Maybe it was so we wouldn't mess with them!"

But what happens between ages four and ten that makes some kids lose this natural wonder about life? Why was the foster son I mentioned so content not to question? Certainly, environment has a lot to do with it. Are a child's questions joyfully answered—well, at least most of the time? Is any question okay to ask, nothing off-limits if asked quietly or privately? Parents can stimulate curiosity in ways besides answering questions. Just talk about the caterpillar or whatever else that pokes by.

I once interviewed my children and several of their friends for a radio program I used to work on. I had hoped they would show the thoughtful, imaginative ideas they come up with when they play. But in a group and in front of a microphone, they just copied one another. Already they were becoming like adults, giving the answers they thought I wanted to hear. By the time we reach adulthood, we've heard the questions and the "right" answers so many times that it becomes difficult to do much original thinking. What does it take to experience life with wonder?

When I was pregnant with our third child, I dragged my slightly dated maternity clothes from a storage box and tried them on. Four-year-old Michelle could hardly contain her excitement. "*Now* you look pregnant-er!" she exclaimed.

"It was much more exciting when I was pregnant for the *first* time—with you," I told Michelle.

"Well, you should still be excited because now you have us, and we're excited," she said thoughtfully.

Sharing With Others

Let's face it: life is often even less exciting than maternity clothes the third time around. But maybe Michelle revealed a secret to restoring childlike wonder—the beauty of sharing an experience with someone else. How might you reach out?

Perhaps you could invite the new employee at work for dessert some evening. Are there international students in your community who could use a friend? Visit some grand-parents whose own children live far away. Take someone shopping who doesn't ordinarily get out. You'll find a fresh perspective and a release from ordinary routine.

Robert Baker is a columnist I enjoy. A science teacher before he recently retired, he once commented that the love notes he intercepted in class didn't bother him too much. Love notes are to be expected in the seventh grade. It was finding notes like "School is boring," or "This class is boring" that disturbed him most. And then one day he found a note that zeroed in: "Mr. Baker is boring."

But it was the recurring theme "*Life* is boring" that really stopped him. Sure, science class can be dull, but at thirteen or fourteen years of age a kid should have zillions of other opportunities that make life exciting. And, as Baker pointed out, we can't shrug off his unofficial findings about bored adolescents when we look at rising teenage suicide rates.[1] Losing childlike wonder can ultimately lead to losing the will to live.

Monotony

Boredom isn't only a problem of young teenagers. Adults drink alcohol because they're bored and it's a way to have fun. Sometimes we watch TV because life is flat and we think there isn't anything else to do. From TV we learn that the solution to a fizzless life is using a plastic charge card to buy happiness. Daily routines, familiar jobs, the same old faces can be "boring" if we let them become that way. No one likes to be around someone who is bored with life.

Sameness is one cause of boredom. My children and I visited my parents for three weeks one summer. When we returned home, I was surprised at how well the children played with their toys, playhouse and swings. It was like

---

[1]Robert Baker, *Christian Living*, May 1985, p. 17.

Christmas morning—everything seemed new.

Much of life's beauty and glory fades with daily contact. When you move to a new area, features like mountains and rivers or monuments and buildings stand out, and you want to photograph everything. In a few short months, you become so accustomed to the scenery that you no longer feel like snapping pictures.

As we think about the importance of restoring wonder, go back with me to the circus, to the row of frosty topped seniors from the nursing home. That my youngsters were captivated by the magic of the circus really wasn't so special. To paraphrase an old saying, "For a child to possess the gift of wonder is a work of nature; for an old person to have it is a work of art." For all of us, the gift of wonder is ultimately a gift of God. As we spread that gift, we share in the work of God.

Specific Tips:

1. Restore your sense of wonder by feeding your inner self. Find some time to meditate—even just ten minutes before anyone else gets up.

Do what you like best: read the Bible, perhaps a psalm, or study a favorite author. Find a quiet spot in the house to be alone. Put on a treasured record and be still before God and yourself.

2. Look at life through other eyes. Maybe a lunch alone at a run-down diner or a hospital snack shop would help you see into a different world. (At a hospital it is often possible to overhear conversations about people who are sick, or exuberant about the birth of a child.) Try sitting in a bus station a few hours. Or standing in an unemployment or welfare line, even though you have a job and plenty to eat.

3. Look at things through a child's eyes. If you have children of your own at home, take time to listen and to

probe. Squat to a child's level and see how a department store or a playground looks. Let the child choose a day's activity. If you don't have children at home, do the same with a niece or nephew or grandchild, or children of friends. Join Big Brothers/Big Sisters, or volunteer to help out with a boys' or girls' club.

IF FRIENDSHIP COMES HARD, DOES GOD STILL LOVE ME?

CHAPTER EIGHT

A secretary at our office used to say her four-year-old girl sometimes announced before they went out, "I'm going to be *shy* tonight." In contrast, most adults don't purposely decide to be shy. At school, church, work, parties, the shy person feels left out—unliked, unwanted, not valued.

A shy person suffers all sorts of inner turmoil, sometimes with physical reactions. Blushing, perspiring, butterflies in the stomach, increased pulse and a pounding heart are some common signals, says one doctor. So when we say someone is painfully shy, that's literally true!

But the way other people view that shyness is the real rub. Often shy persons are seen as "condescending, aloof, bored or hostile," or "unmotivated, ignorant and emotionally cold," says a *Psychology Today* article.[1] Changing these stereotypes is difficult, although Garrison Keillor (of Prairie Home Companion fame) has glorified shyness almost to the point of making it stylish.

I assume that if you're reading this book you probably don't see yourself as the life of the party. Most of us feel the

---

[1]Philip Zimbardo, Paul A. Pilkonis, and Robert M. Norwood, "The Social Disease Called Shyness," *Psychology Today*, May 1975, p. 70.

discomfort of shyness at one time or another. And that becomes a real problem in making friends.

What Is Shyness?

A few years ago a professor at Stanford University did some fascinating studies on shyness. Out of 2,000 persons surveyed, more than 40 percent labeled themselves "shy"![2]

Most of us are neither agonizingly shy nor fearlessly outgoing. After some thirty-five years, I have come to the place where I realize that I'll never be a social butterfly. Nonetheless, I still long to open up more to others. Shyness isn't the worst personal problem in the world. Some even feel it's more of a virtue. A shy person is often discreet, introspective and thoughtful. A shy person may be a good listener, and certainly wouldn't have the problem of intimidating others. But shyness can be a stumbling block in relationships, because shy people are often misunderstood.

Shyness ranges from mere social awkwardness in a crowd, to panicking at the thought of speaking to a group, to extreme repulsion at being touched or touching others.

A team of American psychologists made an interesting observation when they visited China. They reported "observing *no* shy children among the thousands they saw in schools, nurseries, and child care centers."[3] In China, working for personal success is unknown. Everything is done for the group. While such a system has its weaknesses, the absence of shyness seemed to suggest that where individual success is unimportant, there's less need to feel inferior or shy.

In American culture, on the other hand, Little League coaches scream small team members into tears, kids compete for college scholarships, and jobs depend on making a

---

[2]Arthur C. Wassmer, Ph.D., "Seeing Through Shyness," *Family Health*, March 1979, p. 34.

[3]"The Significance of Shyness," *Intellect*, September-October 1975, p. 81.

good first impression. Heavy emphasis on competition may foster poise and perseverance for some people, but how many kids suffer shyness for years because of always being chosen last?

So culture contributes to shyness. A tendency to be bashful or reserved can also be seen in life's transition periods—like adolescence. I went through a time as a teenager when I think I was unhealthily shy. After church on Sunday mornings, I hid in the restroom rather than engage in polite chitchat until my parents were ready to go home! At pajama parties even my closest friends had to prod me to talk: "Come on, Melodie, why don't you talk? What do *you* think about Joe?" I was usually *full* of private thoughts, some so deep that by the time I brought them to the surface to articulate, conversation had moved to another topic. This is often a problem with quiet people.

Psychologists disagree whether shyness is innate or learned. Alexandar Thomas and Stella Chase researched children's temperaments and identified certain children as "slow to warm up" from the earliest days. As babies, they tended to respond to a new food by letting it dribble out of their mouths. In nursery school, they preferred to watch rather than participate in group activities.[4]

Christians aren't immune from shyness. In spite of the fact that we have prayer and the strength of God as a resource, that doesn't seem to help much when it comes to putting our mouths in gear in new situations. In fact, a feeling of "being different" or "not accepted" for having Christian beliefs can contribute to our shyness. Certainly, bonds of commonality and feelings of acceptance with other Christians can help us break out of shyness—but not always.

Familiar Patterns

Experiences of withdrawing and feeling left out contribute to a pattern of shyness. But whatever the cause, shyness

---

[4]*Parents*, August 1987, p. 196.

can be modified so that persons learn to feel more comfortable around others.

For example, Peter Put-Down constantly stops himself from relating to people by a stream of negative thoughts about himself. "I'm not as witty as that guy—or good-looking, or talented." And so, he holds back.

Betty Backwards knows she doesn't have good conversational skills. From past experience, she knows people wander away from a lively group when she starts telling her favorite joke for which she can never remember the punchline.

Dottie Doormat has never learned to stand up for herself, and so others figure she's shy. Inside, she's raging with bright comments, candid comebacks and splendid insights—but she's too scared to get them out.

How to Cope

Since there are many other types of shyness besides these, it's best to focus on the specific skills a shy person lacks. For instance, if interviewing for a job gives you the shakes, learn how to handle an interview. Or if you lack conversational skills, a number of good techniques will help you start conversations with new people. Keep in mind that some of these won't sound comfortable to you, but you can pick and try the ones that work for you.

To start a conversation, try a simple introduction. Tell where you live, what you do, how many children you have. Or give a compliment. At a party, ask the hostess for the recipe for a dish served.

Request some help. Ask the time, for directions to another room or building, or for someone to explain their view of a recent event. Do something nice for someone else— bring a drink or refreshments, or get rid of used plates. But once you start a conversation, how do you keep it going?

A proven method is to get the other person talking about

himself: "You say you're a social worker. What kinds of people do you see?" Avoid asking questions with yes/no or one-word answers. Then become an involved listener. In a conversation, a shy person feels she has to come up with something witty, exciting or at least interesting, when the most important part of being a good conversationalist is careful, appreciative listening. If the person says something you don't understand, ask for an explanation. Respond with further questions about what was just said. For instance, if the social worker says she works primarily in finding foster homes and doing home studies, then you can ask about the requirements for a foster home, or what a home study entails.

Or you might try giving a genuine compliment, a classic Dale Carnegie technique. Everyone likes to hear praise—if it isn't canned. A compliment is a sure way to make a good first impression and focus on the other person. Ironically, the person who gets others talking about themselves is often considered a brilliant conversationalist.

As with any other skill, it takes repeated attempts and real effort to become the conversationalist you'd like to be. At first, some of the practice may seem artificial—just like drilling scales on the piano is an artificial way to play piano. With time and practice, these skills will become part of your own personal style.

To become a good listener, study some of your favorite interviewers on TV. Of course, a journalist's purposes are often different from those of someone engaged in private conversation. But look to see whether the interviewer's questions flow with the direction of the conversation, or if the interviewer seems glued to a list of questions. Is the host interested in the guest, or in making herself look good?

Pastors, counselors and teachers can also teach good listening skills. At our church, we asked our pastor to lead us in a mini-seminar on being better listeners.

Remember "Shy Di"? We hardly think of Princess

Diana as shy anymore—we see her as the confident, gracious, composed young mother of the future King of England. Princess Diana is just one example of how a shy person can change if he or she really wants to. Of course, "Shy Di" had lots of help: briefing sessions in royal protocol, plenty of experience in meeting the glare of lights and cameras, and some of the world's most glamorous gowns to bolster her confidence. And maybe it was only the media image that changed. But ordinary people can shed the image of shyness too. It's *okay* to be shy, but many people are shyer than they like!

It comes down to changing your attitude. A chronically shy person blames himself for social awkwardness, while the non-shy person blames the situation. Susan thinks, "What will people think of me stammering around like this? I'm so dumb!" In contrast, Andrea says, "Well, as soon as I get through this speech, I'll be fine. I suppose even Barbara Walters gets nervous before an interview."

One clinical psychologist sums it up this way: "Shyness is what you *do*, not what you *are*."[5] In other words, shyness is something you can change and control.

Specific Tips:

1. Try saying hello this week to three people you don't know. Then pat yourself on the back!

2. Start one conversation in a non-threatening situation like standing in line at the supermarket, doctor's office, or at the bank. Start by making a comment on the experience you are sharing: "The line here is pretty quick today, isn't it?" Or, "I had a terrible time parking. Do you know any good places?" (Be prepared for those who'd rather not start up a conversation, or who are ready to launch a barrage of complaints. Use good sense!)

---

[5]Wassmer, op. cit., p. 34.

3. Practice using "open" body language to show your interest in other people. Smile. Uncross your arms or legs, and perhaps lean toward the other person. This says that you're really interested in what he or she is saying. Touch, if it seems appropriate. And above all, use good eye contact. (Tips from *Family Health*, p. 34.)

4. Read Eph. 3:16–21 for strength to implement the above tips. Claim the verses for your own. You might want to memorize the benediction in 20–21.

SURVIVAL SKILLS FOR HANDLING CRITICISM

CHAPTER NINE

Rog and Julie were at an informal neighborhood party. Rog expressed some political views loudly as if he were an authority on the subject. Julie was embarrassed, but decided to save her criticism till she got home. On the way home, Julie told Rog what had bothered her.

He listened, then said quietly, "Julie, I'm beginning to feel like you're my mother or my teacher. Like I'm getting a report card each time we go out."

That's a legitimate complaint. Rog had gotten the message that Julie was waging an all-out war to change his behavior, and he reacted humanly.

We resist change—especially when it's forced on us by another person. However, we do change, often gradually, imperceptibly; and other people in our lives *do* influence us. Criticism that is given in love, received in love, and not constantly repeated can help make us better persons. Criticism should be given privately, never in a way that causes an embarrassing scene. And it should always stress the fact that an action or attitude is being criticized, not the person.

In the Bible, Jesus paints a humorous picture of a man standing half-blind with a log in his own eye, trying to get a splinter out of another man's eye (Matt. 7:3–5). It's so much easier to pick at the faults of others rather than conscientiously work on our own shortcomings.

Jesus also says that the measure we use to judge others is the measure by which we ourselves will be judged (Matt. 7:1–2). The implication is that if we are generous and loving toward others, then others will be generous toward us. I think it really works!

One good thing about being a writer is that you learn to take criticism in stride—or change careers! A writer hears criticism of her work as often as a dentist has to listen to dumb jokes about "looking down in the mouth." One mark of a beginning writer is that he or she says, "Look, this is the way I want it to sound, and I will not change a single word!"

Still, criticism is never easy to take, though I find it much easier to listen to criticism about my writing than, for example, about my child-rearing.

We simply hate to be criticized. Some instinct within us recoils, like a cat with an arched, angry back, or a porcupine with prickly, protective quills. It's human nature to not like criticism—but it's also human nature to criticize the actions of others. And often we're the hardest on those we love most!

For instance, when Meg explodes with a list of grievances she's been harboring against her husband, John shows his hurt. Instantly, Meg backs off: "Oh, honey, I'm sorry. I didn't mean all that."

"Yes, you meant it or you wouldn't have said it," John huffs.

"Well, I did mean it, I guess," decides Meg. "But I didn't want to *hurt* you." From there Meg and John can go on to talk about what's been bugging Meg, once John is sure he's not being *personally* attacked.

Learning to give and take criticism is a fine art, a significant secret of friendship. Skill is required because some people melt to tears from as little as a cross look. They interpret everything through the same mindset: *The world is out to get me—I've got to protect myself at every turn.* Such people may have many fine, beautiful traits, but they are difficult to live with.

Of course, there may be a myriad of reasons why a person reacts in an overly sensitive manner—one of which might be my own *in*sensitivity. Perhaps that's one question I can ask myself if I'm caught in a touchy relationship with a friend or acquaintance: Am I insensitive to my friend's feelings, hurts and needs? Do people always seem to fry when I try to offer helpful criticism?

Giving Criticism

If you have a friend or relative who is extremely sensitive, it may help to try to understand the reasons behind his or her reaction. Family background, a battered self-image or loss of a job or marriage partner can all cause a person to wear a thick protective shell. Underneath, though, a sensitive person may be lonely and hurting.

I remember well a time when I was twelve or thirteen. A young girl was playing the piano on television. I had taken piano lessons for years, but didn't practice very faithfully and consequently never played well. But my whole family was praising this young pianist. I said something snooty like, "Well, *I* don't think she's very good."

I remember feeling justified in what I said and that I was more discerning than my family. I really didn't think the young player was good. Furthermore, I became defensive when my family said I was being too critical. "*I'm* not too critical," I retorted. "I'm just saying what I think."

Now I know that I was probably more jealous than discerning and that I spoke from guilt for not having had the discipline to practice piano like I should have. We often criticize others in areas where we feel inadequate ourselves. If I'm overweight, I ridicule others who eat too much. If

I'm jealous of the new neighbor with the pretty face and just-so house, I condemn her for being overly concerned about her looks and her home.

If I'm prone to criticize I need to ask myself, "Could I go and say this to the person's face?" Or, "What good will I do by saying what I'm about to say?" A well-rounded person who feels good about herself doesn't need to bolster her ego by putting down her neighbors or co-workers. Criticism is often a form of defense.

Sometimes it's important to be critical. It isn't all bad. We need to be discerning. If a new clothing style that everyone is raving about (and buying) is pure junk, you can use good judgment and not wear it. Broadcasting your opinion probably won't help and certainly won't endear you to anyone. That's critical discernment in a small thing, but it also applies to other facets of life. And it all stems from a basic good feeling about yourself—about who you are, what you like and what you want to become.

If you are in a position of any kind of responsibility, whether in the home with your children, in a classroom or in an office, at times you must criticize the work, actions and attitudes of others. It's a part of your job. The test is handling it in a healthy, upbuilding way.

Giving effective criticism or feedback may mean learning some new skills. Subjective, general criticisms that are hard to nail down are ineffective in achieving desired results. For instance, a parent telling a child, "You never do anything right," is not only too general, but also carries a moral judgment of "badness."

It is better to give specific feedback, such as, "It would be easier and faster to clean this way." If at work you must tell a co-worker he is doing something incorrectly, say, "It's inefficient or ineffective to do it this way," rather than, "It's wrong to do it this way." For instance, it's probably not wrong to fail to hand in a report on time, but it is wrong to betray a confidentiality. It is, however, *inefficient* to miss the deadline for the report.

Subjective, general criticisms are aggravating, and seldom bring about change anyway.[1] On the other hand, objective, specific and easily demonstrated criticisms can be effective learning tools and lead to quicker changes.

Receiving Criticism

The very word "criticism" has a negative, harsh sound to it. But criticism can be positive as well as negative. It means "to evaluate the merits and faults of." Movie, art and book critics, as everyone knows, often applaud a work they're "criticizing." So the real trick in facing criticism is to view it as something positive. Try to tear down any walls you have built against criticism itself. As someone has said, "The difference between *coaching* and *criticism* is your attitude."[2]

Some criticism is easy to shrug off. If someone reprimands you unjustly or doesn't have his facts straight, you can just say, "I'm sorry you see it that way, but there is more to it than that." But genuine criticism given sensitively still isn't easy to swallow. So how can you put criticism to work for you?

The normal, healthy reaction to even helpful criticism is a slight tinge of hurt, or perhaps embarrassment. We don't like to be caught with our true selves showing. After the initial smart subsides, it's normal to feel angry and defensive: "She doesn't know what she's talking about!" Or, "Who is *he* to criticize me?" It's instinct to want to protect ourselves and our egos.

After these initial negative reactions, learn what you can from the criticism. Can you say "thank you" for the tip? It may be a problem you already knew you had, such as always interrupting people.

If you are criticized at work for not completing a job

---

[1]*Salt and Pepper* (Grand Rapids: Baker Book House, 1974), p. 40.
[2]*The Secretary*, Ann Roberts, October 1977, p. 6.

correctly, don't excuse yourself or blame it on the other guy. If a boss corrects you in a genuine, helpful spirit, you can look at the bright side: Your boss feels you have potential worth developing. She wants to see you improve and feels you can do it.

Self-criticism

As you learn to use criticism constructively and to respond to it graciously, be kind to yourself as well. Alice insists on tearing herself down mentally, as well as in front of others. "I'm no good at speaking in front of groups," she complains, and goes on to describe the dreary details of shaky knees and sweaty palms. Alice even embarrasses her friends in the process, because they certainly don't know how to respond. And it only reinforces her negative image of herself.

Accepting our own weaknesses with grace and tact is as important to friendship as accepting the weaknesses of others. The best part is that we can work and grow if we really want to.

Specific Tips:

1. The next time someone criticizes you, try saying thank you—if you can say it with genuine gratefulness.

2. Think of someone overly sensitive to criticism, who is prone to take things the wrong way. Find out what you can about his or her background.

3. Can you remember a recent critical remark directed toward you? Analyze whether it was poorly stated (i.e., "It is wrong . . ." or "Why can't you do anything right. . . ?"). Rephrase the statement to make it more effective criticism.

4. This week, try stopping yourself in the act of gossiping.

SOMETHING BETTER THAN LETTING IT ALL HANG OUT

CHAPTER TEN

For many years, anger was an emotion that nice people pretended not to have. Then along came therapists who urged people to "let it all hang out." It's best to vent your anger, they said. If you've tried both approaches, you know that neither seems to help relationships!

Anger vented without concern for the feelings of other people is usually hurtful. It can shatter a relationship. Denied or unrecognized anger, on the other hand, prevents true healing from occurring. As we travel the path of becoming the friend we want to be, many of us face a roadblock in dealing with anger. Anger can destroy all that is dear to us: family, friends, job, property.

Negative Associations

If you need convincing that anger has plenty of negative associations, try this quick test with a group of friends. Ask what comes to mind when they think of the word anger. In a church school class the responses were "mad, upset, bad, violence, shouting, silence, nasty, upset stomach, fear, temper, frustration, hot, red, tears, stress" and "throwing things." You get the idea. Only belatedly did someone add "justified" to the list of descriptions of anger.

The word "anger" comes from an old Norse word spelled A-N-G-H, which is pronounced as if someone were clearing his throat: Angh. Not a very pleasant-sounding word. In the ancient Hebrew language, there were various words translated into the English as "anger," such as *chemah*, "hot," and *gharah*, "to burn" or "to glow."

I found these ancient associations fascinating in thinking about our modern understanding of anger. Anger is uncomfortable to experience within ourselves. It is also troubling to be the cause of someone else's anger.

In a role play, two church members acted out an argument. Even though I knew they were only pretending, I found myself looking away, embarrassed to watch. The expressions of anger made me very uncomfortable. A *real* conflict makes me feel the same way, only more so.

Under Attack

Very simply, when we feel anger we feel threatened, like we have no value. Did you ever wonder why discussions about politics or religion rouse so much anger? It's because some of our innermost, heartfelt beliefs are attacked.

Anger is *only* a feeling, not a behavior. So there is nothing wrong with anger in and of itself. What is potentially harmful or helpful is our *response* to anger, our resultant behavior. The Bible cautions us, "If you become angry, do not let your anger lead you into sin." The writer adds, "And don't stay angry all day" (Eph. 4:26, TEV, paraphrased). In other words, unresolved anger festers and grows. I've learned from experience that anger feeds on itself. If I don't deal with it, I get angrier and angrier until I eventually explode.

An example: I suppose all children have trouble keeping their rooms clean. Most of the time I can live with it, closing my eyes when I walk through the door or calmly helping them to pick up and straighten. But now and then it's too much to face, and I erupt with irate words like: "Do you really like to live in this pigpen?!"

What, besides their room, is under attack in this situation? Why does their room threaten me so? That chaotic room exasperates me because it makes me feel they don't respect their demands on my time and energy. Perhaps deep down I dread they'll grow up to be slobs. So my own self-esteem is threatened, a condition which lurks behind much anger.

What makes you angry? A road-hogging driver? Another news story of child abuse? How about a bowling partner who turns every friendly game into a tournament finale?

Becoming Aware

Anger is anger, though there are different levels of intensity. If you want to get a handle on what makes you angry, try keeping an "anger journal." Become conscious of when you feel your temperature rising. Once a day or week, write down the circumstances leading to an outburst. I've learned that I become the most frustrated with others when I'm tired or stressed or have just received an unexpected bill in the mail. Weather might affect your anger level, as teachers often notice in their classrooms.

In keeping your journal, write down how you handled the situation, and somehow indicate the degree of anger you felt. Someone who prides herself on never getting angry may find herself "irritated," "peeved" or "disgusted" many times a week, yet refuse to call it anger. Unacknowledged anger shows up in other ways as well: headaches, sleepless nights, indigestion. Try to discern whether anger is causing any of these problems in your life.

Perceptions and Anger

We've already explored how anger is a response to a threat to ourselves or something dear to us. In the book *How to Live With—and Without Anger,*[1] psychologist Albert Ellis says that our *perceptions* of others influence how angry we become. For example, a friend who good-naturedly calls you a jerk gets a different response than a driver who gestures and mouths "You jerk!" at you on the freeway. Anger, then, is partly a response to the person involved as well as the situation. Thus it's accurate to say that we anger ourselves, rather than others making us angry.

Another type of thinking that feeds anger, says Ellis, is assuming or inventing motives for other people. Once when our part of the country had the biggest blizzard of the year, no one in my family called—even after the storm was featured on the national news. I was miffed. "No one cares about us out here in Virginia!" my mind churned. I began to wonder why they might be mad at us. Finally, I called Mom. She'd been so busy she hadn't seen either the morning or evening news, so she knew nothing about our blizzard. Naturally, Mom was interested and concerned, but just unaware. How often we read between the lines erroneously, with misunderstanding as a result.

Anger also intensifies when we let ourselves off easy, yet treat others harshly. Dave called his friend to help him move some furniture. "Boy, he didn't sound too wild about helping," Dave told his wife as he got off the phone.

"Well," she replied, "I seem to remember a certain man a few weeks ago who grumbled about having to give up an evening to go help his friend."

"That was completely different," Dave muttered.

Do you see the problem? Dave's anger came from being hard on his friend while excusing his own unwillingness to sacrifice.

And finally, Ellis notes, we become angry by personalizing actions or events. A friend keeps us waiting twenty

---

[1] I am indebted to Dan Grandstaff and Donna Barber, teachers of a church school class on anger, for notes from Albert Ellis's book on anger, as well as for many of the other examples in this chapter.

minutes for a lunch appointment and we say, "I can see how much I count with her." In truth, your friend may have simply scheduled her day too full, and may need a seminar on time management!

If we stop to listen to our anger, we often spot some of these distorted modes of thinking. Try to discern what's really behind your anger. It's sort of a variation on the old "count-to-ten" technique. Often we gain new insight that can help us understand and resolve our fury.

Women and Anger

Women in particular may have trouble admitting or expressing anger effectively, says Harriet Goldhor Lerner in *The Dance of Anger*. Our social conditioning is crucial in understanding anger. Loud discussions may not cause discomfort in an all-male group. Women, in contrast, are taught to speak softly and to blame themselves rather than admit anger.

We fear the price of expressing anger: losing a mate, alienating a parent, hurting a friend. Lerner hastens to warn that merely *venting* anger doesn't bring change. In fact, it can even reinforce the old patterns in a relationship, making it more difficult for change to occur.

"Anger is a signal, and one worth listening to,"[2] says Dr. Lerner. Anger tells us something is wrong. Sometimes others imply that our anger isn't legitimate, as in "She's just irrational." But *any* anger is worth examining.[3]

Break the Cycle

Discussions sometimes just go round and round. How can we break out of self-defeating cycles of anger? Lerner suggests some basic do's and don'ts. For starters, do speak

[2]Harriet Goldhor Lerner, *The Dance of Anger* (New York: 1985).
[3]Ibid., p. 1.

up when an issue is important. If staying silent costs you bitterness, then speaking up is far better. The worst time to talk, though, is while you're really fuming. We often need space before we can present our real concern or know what actually angers us. Count to ten or one hundred. Do, however, try to clear up misunderstandings before too much time goes by.[4] The Bible says, "Don't let the sun go down on your wrath" (Eph. 4:26). That's another way of saying, "Don't let it fester."

If anger has threatened a relationship, try to clarify the real issues. Surface blowups often cloud deeper feelings of being treated unfairly. We all know it's self-defeating to use below-the-belt tactics like blaming, labeling, and ridiculing. Most of us use them anyway and apologize later. But if you catch yourself going for the jugular, stop! Hurt can go deep, and wounds take time to heal.

What do you do when your insides are ready to explode? "I just can't help it," says Sue. "When Roger comes home late for supper without calling me, I'm ready to boil. I try to be understanding and not get mad, but it seems like the anger just has to come out."

Anger is a natural, human emotion. Everyone gets angry. At times anger protects us, telling us where relationships may need mending. But it isn't inevitable for us to *blow up* periodically, like Old Faithful.

Try to look at the situation objectively. Sue can tell herself, "Roger probably thought that calling would delay him that much longer, or maybe he just forgot. I guess I'm upset because I don't like over-done suppers, and his not calling makes me feel like he's still a little boy. I'll eat and just let his supper get cold. Maybe that will help him remember in the future!"

This kind of objectivity is hard to maintain when we're angry. But if we practice listening to our anger, figuring out

---

[4]Ibid.

what is at the bottom of it, we can find ways to cope before we lose control.

Specific Tips:

1. If you catch yourself becoming angry this week, count to ten and look at why you're angry. Accept and acknowledge it, and see if you can find a way to rationally discuss your feelings at a later time.

2. Retrace your patterns of anger over the past several months. Do you see any similarities?

3. Using a concordance, look up biblical references to anger, for instance, Matt. 5:23–24. What does it/doesn't it say?

THOU SHALT KEEP THY PATIENCE

CHAPTER ELEVEN

Aren't you glad God didn't send Moses down from the mountain with a commandment like, "Thou Shalt Keep Thy Patience"? Even Moses would have promptly disobeyed that rule (read how he crashed the stone tablets when he found his people had built the golden calf, Ex. 32:1–20). Of course, Moses' impatience was justified—but so is mine sometimes.

But as I work on this chapter, the title makes me especially uncomfortable. These last few days, I have hardly been the master of patience: the transmission on the car went out; the transformer on the TV burned up; we're rushing into the Christmas season with this book due six days after Christmas (remind me never to sign a contract for December 31 again!). All this on top of normal job and housekeeping duties. Is that why the children's playfulness sometimes sends me over the edge these days? Once again, justice sees to it that what I write preaches to *me* first and foremost.

Patience, I believe, comes hard for most of us, but it is vital to healthy friendships. Whether it's dieting, waiting for the subway or hearing from the bedroom yet another request for a drink of water, few of us are masters of patience all of the time.

An Impatient Society

Impatience is built into our culture. We speak highly of young executives who climb to the top *fast*. We don't like long waits for individually prepared meals, so we gobble down mass-produced *fast* food. The young couple feels as if they need a color TV, dishwasher and stereo *fast*.

Since our society exalts the very opposite of patience, is it any wonder that examples of rudeness and impatience abound? On the other hand, have you ever noticed the un-hurriedness with which most toddlers approach life? A two-year-old wanders along, taking time to squat and observe an ant scurrying across the sidewalk. She pauses to hunt for an airplane in the sky. Four-year-old Tanya is adept at spotting bird "nestes" (as she calls them) as we drive along. When have I had time to look for bird nests? The toddler smells a flower, and likes looking all around at the people in a res-taurant more than concentrating on her food. Mommy urges, "Hurry up and eat, dear," or "Can't you walk a little faster?"

And the very next day it's the toddler's turn to be im-patient: "I want a glass of milk, and I want it now!" exclaims Megan to Mom, who has her arms full of laundry. No won-der children learn to be impatient when they have such per-fect role models!

Most of us can be patient when we *want* to be. Consider the fishing enthusiast, waiting hours for a bite. Or remember the old ritual of getting a tan. I never would have enjoyed lying in the hot sun for hours on end, perspiring and being uncomfortable, if someone had *made* me do it.

If you are impatient and want to learn more control, think of an area where you already have exemplary patience. For instance, perhaps you can decorate a cake, or add col-umns of figures with the utmost endurance. When hearing the same question five times from your three-year-old sends you up the wall, remember that raising a child is infinitely more important than making a picture-perfect cake. Putting things in perspective can help you have a little more tolerance.

I was intrigued by the synonyms for "patient" listed in a dictionary of synonyms: *submissive, resigned, uncomplaining, passive.* These are qualities that aren't exactly prized in our present society. Certainly, no one enjoys being a doormat, as these words imply.

Find a Balance

Where is the balance, then, between being too quick to snap and being too resigned to say anything? I remember reading how the press made a big deal of Princess Diana's refusing to pose for pictures on one of her ski trips as a newlywed. Papers and TV called her "spoiled." But put yourself in her shoes: pursued on *every* outing by hordes of photographers, *never* left to a private moment. Was she too quick to snap?

Putting yourself in the other person's shoes is a good exercise whenever you're faced with someone who's boiling. Try to imagine why that person has run out of patience. It may be obvious—like the clerk checking out a long line of customers at closing time. Or the source of impatience may be more hidden—a stressful marriage, a sick child or an unemployed spouse.

The biggest benefit in learning patience is that it makes us more likeable. Another reward is simply being pushed beyond our former limits of endurance. It's like exercise. We only develop strength and stamina when we drive ourselves for that extra lap or that extra five minutes of exercise. In the same way, practicing patience when we don't feel like it helps us develop strength to deal with stress. Cultivating patience in the little things can help us gain perspective for the long haul.

Practice Makes Patience

How do we develop patience? I find I'm more impatient when I'm tired, too busy or under stress—like at the beginning of this chapter. The solution to this kind of impatience is, of course, to get rest or relief from the stress. Plus, I've found that merely putting my finger on the problem—giving it a name—helps to defuse my impatience.

Another way to learn to be more patient is to prepare in advance for situations certain to be frustrating. If I'm headed to a big clearance sale at a department store, I tell myself, "Okay. There's going to be lots of people, noise and confusion." I ready myself for long lines and short tempers. Then it's easier to take it all in stride.

Another remedy for impatience may sound strange: regular exercise. One management specialist notes that anyone in a high-stress profession is especially prone to impatience—for instance, a waiter who has to deal with swarms of rude customers.[1] Exercise releases tension and can actually affect the chemical balances in our bodies.

The pace of today's life, the overcrowding of our highways and the anonymity of modern society all contribute to a tendency to impatience. If I know I'll probably never again see the people standing in line at the supermarket, I may be more tempted to try to break in the line. If I haven't developed any friendships with the people in my building, why worry about being rude in the elevator?

Some lines in James 1:2–4 give incentive for practicing patience: "Consider it pure joy . . . when you face trials of many kinds, because you know that the testing of your faith develops perseverance," or on-going patience. The Bible continues: "Perseverance must finish its work so that you may be mature and complete, not lacking anything." While these verses refer specifically to growth in faith, I think they

---

[1]*U.S. News & World Report*, August 22, 1983, p. 55.

show how patience helps build our character to enhance relationships.

Take an everyday circumstance like getting behind a pokey driver on a busy, narrow road. Our first impulse is to pass as quickly as possible. If that's impossible we fume and fuss, even though we know it won't do any good.

Here's a good chance to practice the art of patience. I can tell myself that the driver has a perfect right to go as slow as he or she wants. If that were my grandmother, would I want other drivers blowing their horns at her? Besides, I'll probably reach my destination about the same time anyway. I'll relax, let my blood pressure return to normal and enjoy the scenery for a change!

At Work

It's one thing to practice patience with a ton of steel between you and the aggravator, and quite another to manage it face to face. What happens when your boss loads on the work? Or your kids need five items for school *right away*?

There are at least two approaches. You can hold your temper and proceed to do what's needed as quickly as possible. You appear composed, but inwardly you boil. Or, you can find a non-threatening way to express what you're feeling. "I'm overloaded right now. Could you help me decide which item has priority? I'll tackle the rest as soon as possible."

Patience With Myself

Sometimes it's hardest to be tolerant of the person I know best of all: myself. As important as it is to keep pushing ourselves to grow, improve and change, it's also important to be patient, allowing ourselves some grace.

For instance, I had been meaning for years to visit a neighbor. You know how days, months and even years can slip by and somehow you never get around to it.

Finally, one evening, I picked up the phone and asked, "Would you like a little company this evening?" I was amazed at how simple it was. But instead of feeling good that I'd *finally* visited this neighbor, I kept chastising myself for taking so long to call.

Mike and Ginny are a young couple who for many years supported themselves only with free-lance writing and photography. As you can imagine, it was hard to make a living without regular paychecks. Yet, they were patient about getting ahead. "It was kind of an apprenticeship period," Mike says, "like the artists who used to work for eight to ten years or more at little or no pay perfecting their craft."

I admire this kind of patience, the dedication that says, "We don't have to be successful or well-to-do as long as we're happy, like what we're doing and feel it's what God wants us to do right now."

It's not always a virtue to be patient. There is a time to be *im*patient as well. As the writer of Ecclesiastes put it, "There is a time for everything . . . a time to be silent and a time to speak" (Eccles. 3:1a, 7b). Yet most of us show too little patience rather than too much. And that keeps many friendships from moving forward.

Friendships often develop over many years, growing, mellowing, building trust. We need patience for the daily irritations in relationships, as well as to nurture relationships long-term.

Specific Tips:

1. If you face a frustrating situation today, rather than steaming and fretting, tell yourself—no matter how ridiculous it sounds—"Here is my chance to *practice* patience."

2. If you have children, examine whether you are unconsciously providing a model of impatience. Think of one time this past week when you were impatient, and one time

your child was. Compare the two incidents. Was your impatience justified? Was your child's?

3. Write down the three situations that cause you to lose your cool the most often. Decide how you can prayerfully deal with each:

a. Talk with other parties involved.

b. Prepare in advance so problems won't arise.

c. Tell yourself, "This too shall pass."

d. Live with it.

4. Someone has said that losing your temper usually causes other people to lose respect for you. In thinking about others, can you think of a time when this was true? Can you think of a time when it was *not* true?

ALL WORK AND NO PLAY

CHAPTER TWELVE

An old verse by an unknown writer is the kind of poem you used to see hanging above many kitchen sinks:

> If your nose is held to the grindstone rough,
> And you hold it down there long enough,
> Soon, you'll say, there's no such thing
> As brooks that babble and birds that sing.
> Three things will all your world compose—
> Just you, the grindstone, and your old nose!

That's why you're reading a chapter on the importance of hobbies in a book on the secrets of friendship. The old saying "All work and no play makes Jack a dull boy" is really true. Hobbies can make us more interesting and relaxed in our relationships.

Isn't it old-fashioned to insist on that? It's the kind of sermon your mother probably used to preach: "You'll be more interesting if you have a hobby. Do something, Johnny!"

Hobbies seem to have little to do with keeping on a fast career track, and certainly it is arduous to find time for hobbies. Who needs one more "have-to" on a to-do list?

The Drudge

Mom was probably wiser than she realized. It turns out that such sayings as "all work and no play" have a sound basis. Scientists now say that it takes both sides of the brain to deal with life in the best possible manner. We know that one side of the brain is more logical and the other side more intuitive. Immersing oneself in a familiar activity—like knitting—that takes little logic or thinking lets the logical side of the brain rest. The brain can therefore be more productive when logical thinking resumes.[1]

If we leave ourselves no reflection time, no time for being frivolous, we block part of the natural process for finding solutions to even mundane problems. It is said that Jane Austen worked out the plots to her classic novels over an evening's sewing with a notebook nearby.[2]

The pattern of taking time for work and rest is part of the creation story. After working six days, on the seventh day God rested. The creation narrative does not describe divine rest, or how long God's days were, but simply that God set aside time for rest.

Since we are made in the image of God, surely we need to set aside time for rest or leisure as well! In *Gift From the Sea*, Anne Morrow Lindbergh says that "nothing feeds the center so much as creative work, even humble kinds like cooking and sewing, baking bread, and weaving cloth."[3]

There was a time when I hadn't thought much about this need. One day at a seminar we were supposed to introduce ourselves by telling about our hobbies. I couldn't think of what to say! I was embarrassed to realize that I occupied most of my spare time with work (writing) or with my chil-

---

[1]Julia Cameron, "My Mother Was Right," *Ladies' Home Journal*, November 1984, p. 22.
[2]Ibid., p. 24.
[3]Anne Morrow Lindbergh, *Gift From the Sea* (New York: Random House, Inc., 1975), p. 53.

dren. Now, I enjoy both writing and the kids, so what's wrong with that?

Then I began to think about a long list of old hobbies: oil painting, guitar playing, needlework, raising house plants, reading, piano playing, flower arranging, bowling. When I became a mother, I cut out most activities in order to concentrate on the children when I was home. That seminar exercise made me realize something had dried up within me (along with my paints and houseplants!). The frivolous, spontaneous "just for me" side of life had become almost nonexistent.

Finding Time

Now I try to find a few minutes a week to resume one old hobby, playing the piano. It's not easy, because the baby wants to "play" the piano then too. But it's not as messy to get out or clean up like painting or needlework. And it's free!

Neither my work, as much as I like it, nor my children, as much as I love them, bring quite the feeling of abandon I get when playing even a mediocre rendition of Beethoven or an old country hymn. Because I'm *not* striving to be a concert pianist or even the church musician, I'm free to stumble along without lofty goals or scheduled practice times.

I'm not saying we shouldn't work to perfect hobby skills. But the best hobby for people who attack everything with intense seriousness is one they're bad enough at that they can never hope to be famous! Some people enlarge their hobbies into a part-time business or income-producing thing, and that's fine. But then the activity probably ceases to be a hobby and becomes work.

At that point, it might be a good idea to pick up a new hobby not done for income, something you do just for you, for the pure hilarity or exhaustion of it. One who enjoys hang-gliding claims, "One good flight is like breathing laughing gas for a week."[4] Joggers talk about the natural high they get from an extended period of running. Fishing enthusiasts sit for hours without catching a thing—just for the "recreation."

Some hobbies demand working or playing with a friend; others can be done alone. I think both are useful. Julia Cameron described how she revived a childhood dream and took horseback riding lessons. She's found herself immersed in new joys, new conversations and new thoughts. While riding and caring for her horse, her problems move to the periphery.[5]

Myrna is learning to quilt and collects antique quilts. She finds her hobby is a conversation-starter and that it provides something specific to do with a friend, like attending a quilt show or auction or hunting down a particular design.

Dave loves to tinker and collect "tinkering equipment," as his wife calls it. He can see something in a store, go home, and make a copy of it without even drawing a plan!

Taking classes can be another outlet. Educator Dr. Ruth Van Doran confirms that there has been a dramatic upswing in learning for learning's sake. She says, "People now come to the university for more enduring satisfactions. . . . People want to have some balance in their lives. They realize the need to mix vocational and avocational interests."[6]

Like our mothers and our friends, Dr. Van Doran believes in hobbies. Hobbies for balance. Hobbies for perspective. Hobbies for enjoyment.

Preparing for Retirement

A major reason for developing or reactivating old hobbies is for a period of life that seems far off to most of us—

---

[4]"New Wave Mountain Men," *Newsweek*, October 1, 1984, p. 83.
[5]Cameron, op. cit., p. 24.
[6]Ibid.

retirement. What will we do when work or family no longer fill most of our waking hours?

Some of the happiest older people I know are those who are able to fill their time with some work or hobby, and who are in frequent contact with others. Wellness experts say that being active and involved even contributes to physical health and long life. Again, we're back to the idea of integrating all of life and keeping a balance. Just as it's important to care for physical, mental and spiritual needs, it's important to develop the emotional. Hobbies contribute to all of life. When I play the piano, for example, my fingers get a workout and my soul gets a lift. Some of my best moments of private worship come from playing the piano.

For Christians who believe that all time is a gift of God, even our leisure time is something to use thoughtfully. Sometimes this means doing *nothing*; sometimes our faith calls us to use our free time to serve others; sometimes it urges us to a wild game of basketball in the driveway with the kids or to bang away on an out-of-tune piano.

Leisure time is meant for relaxing, being renewed, reflecting and being *re-created*! And hobbies can open doors to new friends with whom we already have something in common.

Specific Tips:

1. What would you do if you had a year off from your paid job while someone else paid all your expenses? What would you do if you could do anything you wanted to?

2. Figure out how many of your hours are occupied each day. Include work, commuting, housework, dressing and childcare. (If you're like me, you may have only about an hour that's really free.)

3. Take the activity you listed (number one), and look for ways you could work that activity into your free time (number two). Are there fifteen free minutes here and there

which you could use toward fulfilling a "dream" job, activity or hobby? For instance, I wrote these "specific tips" in a half-hour I had between the time I finished dressing in the morning and the time I needed to wake the kids for school.

IF ONLY I'D BEEN BORN THE OLDEST

CHAPTER THIRTEEN

Have you ever compared notes with a friend: "I was a middle child too!" or "I was the baby"? We usually feel an immediate camaraderie with someone whose family background is similar.

How does birth order affect the development of personality? Does it shape your relationships with others?

There are entire books on the effects of birth order and researchers who devote whole careers to it. But I want to include an introductory look here since birth order seems to influence relationships profoundly.

Characteristics

While there are exceptions to every generalization, one of the first patterns birth order specialists note is that first-born children frequently have a strong leadership bent—they're high achievers. A disproportionately high number of U.S. presidents, for instance, have been *oldest* sons; only three presidents were youngest children.[1] Oldest sons tend

---

[1] James T. Baker, "First-Born Sons and Brothers' Keepers," *Christian Century*, November 22, 1978, p. 1133.

to be heads of corporations and pastors of large churches. On the flip side, almost every presidential assassin we know anything about has been a *little* brother—a later son![2]

I'm reporting research on oldest sons because the most research has been done on that group. This field of study is relatively recent, beginning in earnest only fifty years ago. Much of what has been written and said is thus somewhat theoretical.

Behavioral scientist Alfred Adler was one of the pioneers of birth order studies. He coined the term "dethroned king" to describe the first-born child who suddenly loses his or her monopoly on the parents' attention. This loss often gives the first-born child a life-long need for "recognition, attention, and approval."[3]

Karl Konig supplied further credibility to Adler's theories. Konig, a general practitioner in Germany, noticed that eldest children displayed similar behavioral traits. Second-borns and third-borns also were similar as groups.

Another professor did informal studies on birth order, studying Boston area lawyers, who were typically hard-working, conservative and intelligent. He found that two-thirds were first-borns.[4]

The same professor also studied Rhode Island beauticians. Beauticians are typically friendly, outgoing and easy to talk to. He found that there were more second-borns in this group. When he studied a religious order of nuns he discovered a predominance of third-born children, who seemed to be more withdrawn and artistic.[5]

First-borns tend to be shy, sensitive, ambitious, conscientious, conservative and serious about life. On the other hand, second-borns are perceived as relatively relaxed,

---

[2]Irving Harris, "Little Brother," *Psychology Today*, October 1976, p. 48.

[3]Jack Horn, "What Scholars, Strippers, and Congressman Share," *Psychology Today*, May 1976, p. 34.

[4]Gordon E. Rowley, "How Birth Order Affects Your Personality," *The Saturday Evening Post*, November 1980, p. 62.

[5]Ibid.

cheerful, easy-going, friendly and independent.[6]

Physically, second-born babies on the average are bigger right from the beginning. The size difference often lasts at least into adolescence.[7]

Interestingly, more than social reasons may be responsible for the strong differences between first- and second-born. In a study in the late 1970s, psychologists discovered that hormone levels found in blood samples were significantly higher in first-born children. Elevated hormone levels might partially explain the tendency of first-borns to be high achievers. The age of the mother, weight of the infant or the length of labor could not account for the increased levels, the psychologists said.[8]

Even more intriguing than size and hormonal differences are some general observations about health, popularity and self-esteem. First-borns in adulthood typically seek the care of a doctor quicker than later-borns. (This is probably explained by the habit of parents to run to the doctor faster with a first-born.) Second children frequently fear life in general less than first-borns, and they make good pilots, race car drivers and deep sea divers![9] Second children are often more friendly and playful than first-borns right from infancy.

Many factors can change these characteristics: spacing between children, the death or disability of an older child (moving the second-born into a position of leadership), wealth or poverty, parenting styles, a divorce, or stepchildren coming into the family.

What about a fourth child? Well, the experts differ. Some feel that a fourth child starts the cycle all over again, and has "first-born" characteristics. A fifth becomes a second-born, and so on.

---

[6]Joan S. Weiss, "Your Second Child," *Parents*, August 1981, p. 47.
[7]Ibid., p. 48.
[8]Mary Brown Porlee, "First-Borns Have Higher Hormone Levels," *Psychology Today*, April 1979, p. 102.
[9]Weiss, op. cit., p. 48.

Birth Order and Relationships

You can observe similar patterns by looking at your own acquaintances, but don't take these few statements on birth order and start pigeonholing all your friends! While such analysis may be fun, it won't ever be totally accurate and can even be harmful.

Exceptions and extenuating circumstances always alter personal characteristics, and birth order is only one of many factors that shape your personality. Your own in-born characteristics, environment, the wealth or poverty of your parents, the way your parents raised you—all these contribute. Still, understanding the influence of birth order can sometimes help you understand relationships. For example, maybe your spouse subconsciously reminds you of a nonconformist younger brother. Perhaps a friend irks you because she tries to boss you around—like an older sister?

In the book *First-Born, Second-Born*, Barbara Sullivan describes how two women in her church came to her with a problem. The women had worked together on committees and in outreach for several years and had always been close. But now, Martha was feeling that Patrice was trying to dominate her.

As they talked they discovered that Patrice, as a firstborn daughter, tended to "mother" other women she worked with. As a newcomer in the church, Martha had at first responded well to this mothering. But Martha, a third child, had always felt dominated by her successful first-born sister. Martha had begun to come to terms with her underdog feelings, and was rebelling against Patrice's protectiveness. Patrice and Martha needed to learn to be partners, instead of teacher-student or parent-child. This brought more freedom for both women to exercise their gifts.[10]

Understanding a bit about typical birth order character-

---

[10]Barbara A. Sullivan, *First-Born, Second-Born* (Grand Rapids, Mich.: The Zondervan Corporation, 1983), p. 15–17.

istics helps me to be more accepting of others. If a friend and I get into a tiff, I can give him the benefit of the doubt and say, "Ah, well, he's just a typical third child." For instance, long ago I had a friend who thought nothing of asking for an occasional little loan to tide him over. He was the youngest in a large family, and was well-liked and quite charming. Now I understand that his carefree approach to responsibility was quite normal for a youngest child, and I shouldn't have felt so frustrated or abused when he sponged off me.

Changing the Influences

While our pasts and family birth order may shape us, we're not bound to the past! With God's help we can make radical changes in our lives. How does God let us know about areas where we need to change? Often through other people's subtle and not so subtle remarks and actions. Even a job review can reveal weakness. Family members know us too well, but often we aren't willing to listen to those closest to us. All of these can help us evaluate and change the negative characteristics of our birth order.

One of my favorite examples of radical change is the Old Testament story of Jacob and Esau (Gen. 25—33). These two brothers were twins, so I'm not sure how they fit into birth order analysis. Technically, Esau was the oldest, but he forfeited his position as eldest son when he sold his birthright, then was tricked out of its benefits as well. Jacob, a conniving schemer of a brother, was helped along by an equally wily mother. We read that "Isaac loved Esau, because he ate of his game, but Rebekah loved Jacob" (25:25–28).

To be fair, Rebekah knew God had promised that "the elder shall serve the younger" (25:23), and so she might have thought she needed to help God out. Jacob meant well too, and at least married inside the faith, unlike Esau.

Jacob and Esau become great rivals, and Jacob flees for his life from the understandable wrath of his brother. At Bethel, Jacob has a dream and a "conversion experience," and at last we feel he is on the right track.

Then Jacob is upstaged by an even craftier uncle. After working an unfathomable seven years for the love of his life, Rachel, he wakes up married to her older sister Leah instead! We tend to sympathize with Jacob, forgetting that he is only getting his just reward for the way he tricked his own father. He works another seven years for Rachel, and years later decides to take his prosperous tribe back home. Skeletons from the past make him afraid to meet Esau. He sends gifts ahead, and Jacob—who has struggled all his life to control others—wrestles all *night* with a man (Gen. 32:24). This contender finally throws Jacob's thigh out of joint and gives Jacob a new name, "Israel," and a new inner nature.

At dawn we see Jacob limping (what a beautiful reminder of God's touch, 32:31) to meet the brother he had cheated, bowing to the ground seven times as he advanced. The Bible says, "But Esau ran to meet him, and embraced him, and fell on his neck and kissed him and they wept" (33:4). That's some greeting!

God touched Jacob, a second-born, manipulating, conniving "Mama's boy," and made him the leader of the house of Israel—and a forerunner to Jesus.[11] Through God's touch all of us can surmount the conditions of our birth to become all that He means us to be in our relationships. Praise be to God!

Specific Tips:

1. Compare your childhood/current families to these generalities on birth order.

---

[11] I am indebted to Darrel Hostetler, Bible teacher, for my notes on this study of Jacob.

2. Compare *your* position in the family to the norms presented. What strengths do you possess? How would you like to change?

3. Close your eyes and imagine yourself as the oldest, or the youngest, or an older child. Explore what you would feel differently. For fun, decide to live one day as though you occupied the birth position you always wished you did.

YOU DON'T STOP GROWING WHEN YOU REACH EIGHTEEN

CHAPTER FOURTEEN

Much recent study has focused on developmental stages in adult life. Researchers are finding that adults face transitions and changes that challenge them from age twenty to eighty almost as predictable as the terrible two's and teenage rebellion.

So we don't stop growing when we reach eighteen. I find that fact exciting. As an adult, I'm still changing socially, emotionally and spiritually. To me, that brings new interest to life. Moreover, knowing that some of the upheavals I've experienced are almost universal assures me that I'll get through a particular stage as surely as a toddler eventually gets through diapers.

Knowing a bit of what to expect at various points in life can help us press on, because we realize that we're facing the same challenges as everyone else. If we're forty, for example, we don't have to kill ourselves to keep up with the kids. Few of our peers could do it either. So there is comfort in numbers and in an awareness of what's typical at different stages. Equipped with this knowledge I can better grasp what friends or family members are going through as well.

As we look at various phases, keep in mind that I've

highlighted only a *few* characteristics of the young adult, early adult and middle adult years. Of course, there are many exceptions—people who don't worry about reaching sixty-five, for example—just as there are teenagers who don't rebel. These are general characteristics and age groupings.

Young Adult Years

Achieving independence from family is the first challenge facing most young adults. The typical young adult spends the period between ages eighteen and twenty-nine completing formal education, exploring careers, and often starting a family. Many purchase their first home and find a thrill in planting new trees and a garden.

Betty is representative of this age group. She is twenty years old with a ten-month-old baby—perhaps a bit younger than many first-time mothers these days. Although some parts of her life are fairly settled, her husband is still finishing his schooling. She feels an urgency for Dan to complete his training so they can get on with their lives.

"I just wish I knew if we'll be moving when he finishes school," she says. They are seeking church roots, but uncertainty about what the next year will bring makes them reluctant to get fully involved.

For many, young adulthood is still a period of seeking, experimenting and testing—and sometimes feeling misunderstood. Betty may ask her mother for advice on what to do with ten-month-old Aaron, and then criticize her mom's suggestions. Betty is attempting to find out what's right for herself, to forge her own way and own values.

At the age of twenty-nine, I wrote my first book, *On Troublesome Creek*, which dealt with my struggles and joys as a nineteen-year-old fresh out of high school. It was only through writing that I began to put together some of the pieces of what happened during those years. Self-understanding takes time. Parents need to be patient even with children who are now supposed to be grown up.

Early Adult Years

In the early adult years, from about ages twenty-nine to thirty-nine, career often becomes the main focus of life, sometimes to the extent that old friendships and family are neglected. One young woman commented, "Everyone seems in such a rush. Everything's moving so fast."

Some adults in this stage fulfill church and community obligations only because it will aid in their rise to the top. Tom wants his kids to grow up knowing about God, so he finds himself sitting through Sunday school for the first time in twenty years. He wants his kids to benefit, but he'd rather be reading *The Wall Street Journal* or golfing with his business associates.

Toward the end of the thirties, most in this age group find themselves becoming disturbingly aware of growing older. A softball game at the company picnic leaves its mark for days, and we mourn our passing youth. We feel like we've arrived at the end of a year with little to celebrate.

Middle Adult Years

Mid-life is a time when many persons reevaluate skills and life goals. We're embarrassed to find ourselves stuck again in the position of a teenager, not sure what to do with our lives. Adults are supposed to *know*. Life-planning experts, however, assure us that it's okay not to know. It's okay to pass once again through a period of searching. Those who look at the developmental stages of spirituality add that it's also normal to question faith during crises. As one man wrote, "Where is God when the farm fails?"

Role Model

Sometimes I'm amazed that teens ever survive adolescence. If people in middle adulthood face some of the same turbulence, how are we supposed to cope? More than that, how can we emerge victorious, deeper, more seasoned people?

Think of someone you admire—not a celebrity, but an ordinary person from your neighborhood or school or workplace. What gives her that special edge?

My mind runs to Antoinette "Toni" Bosco, author of *Successful Single Parenting*. I remember that when I was privileged to meet Toni a number of years ago, I could barely believe that she had passed the fifty mark and that she had six grown children.

Toni talked about her divorce, describing what a difficult time she had as a Catholic single parent. But she refused to accept the label "broken" that many cast on her family. Hers was a whole family, because there was love and completeness and acceptance even though the marriage situation had grown intolerable.

In crises, like the time a teenager daughter went hitchhiking against household rules, Toni decided alone what to do. She dared to ground her daughter, but found her a sewing machine so the girl would have something worthwhile to do in all those hours at home. The risk paid off, and that daughter became a fashion designer. That's just one of the joys that lights Toni's face as she talks.

Things might have easily been different for Toni. If she had wallowed in the ruin others predicted for her family, she would have decided that her divorce had produced a no-good hitchhiking daughter. Toni would have heaped guilt on herself and pasted on her family the label "broken"—and concluded that her daughter and the rest of the family were beyond hope. But by growing through her crises, Toni fashioned a vital, animated spirit that makes her fun to be around.

What do you do if middle age finds you less than radiant? Studies of life transitions suggest that we should view middle age as an opportunity to reevaluate what we've done with our lives and to take appropriate steps to change. You've always wanted to go back to school. There's still time. You want to begin an exercise program—go see a doctor, then start one. You want to be more (or less!) involved in your children's lives. Begin this week! None of these new paths will take away the gray hair or give you a higher I.Q., but you'll be more fun to be around and like yourself better, too.

Getting Around to It

I am continually challenged to take these words I write on the secrets of friendship and implement them in my own life.

Relationships took a backseat during the first years of my marriage as I concentrated on my work and my husband. Then Michelle, Tanya and Doreen came along, and "children" became a focus. How do I go about reviving old friendships that have become mere names on a Christmas card list? How do I begin *new* friendships?

By getting to it! In their book *In Search of Excellence*, Thomas Peters and Robert Waterman talk about "bias for action." To apply that buzz phrase to my own goals, I needn't wait until I have a free weekend or until we can replace the dingy drapes in the living room to invite friends over. The time for friendships is now!

Peters and Waterman got their idea for their book on excellence when they walked into the lobby of a hotel they had stayed in only once before. They didn't have reservations and it was late, so they were prepared for a hassle. To their great surprise, the clerk on duty looked up and called them by name. That was their idea of an excellent hotel!

Obviously, it must have taken plenty of effort for that

clerk to remember their names. The same is true of any goal we want to accomplish in our personal life. Making more friends or losing weight doesn't happen suddenly, nor does writing a novel come about without a great amount of effort.

We've probably all admired people who embody this "bias for action," the tendency to get things done. I've observed at least one thing about such people: It's not that they have more energy, or inborn skills or abilities. What makes them different is that they don't worry about all the minor details that impede all of us non-movers and shakers! They put people before worries about age, skills, room decor and even career.

No matter where we are in our life pilgrimage, growth can happen out of disappointment and pain. Life can be good at twenty, forty, sixty and beyond.

What is the secret? An inner life that takes life's crises and learns from each one. The mature adult isn't one who has escaped problems, but rather grown through them. The mature adult doesn't worry about how many friends she can count, but about whether she is a friend others can count on.

Specific Tips:

1. Map out a lifeline for yourself. Draw a line on a long piece of paper and mark off significant eras or events like "college years" or "birth of Amy." Indicate what you've devoted various stages of life to: "Family," "Training," "Career," etc. Assume you'll grow old! *Plan* for what you'd like to focus on in the years to come.

2. Map out the same kind of spiritual chronology of your life thus far. Mark peaks and valleys. What reflections does it cause? Does it help you understand anyone else better? A child? Parent? Friend?

WHEN THE ONLY MESSAGE ON YOUR ANSWERING MACHINE IS FROM YOU

CHAPTER FIFTEEN

I think every mother remembers whom she shared the room with when she was in the hospital to give birth. My first roommate was having her second child. What I remember about her most is a time she told me about herself.

Alice (not her real name) lived in an isolated rural area. After she fixed breakfast and cleaned the house in the morning, she and her first child always went to spend the day at her mother's. She returned home only in time to make supper. I suspect that running home to mom was Alice's attempt to escape the loneliness that at times stalks each of us.

Loneliness is universal. And like Alice, each of us develops coping mechanisms to ward off feelings of friendlessness. Some talk non-stop. One man calls his answering machine each morning from work so a friendly voice will greet him when he gets home. Another hooks up sophisticated electronic gadgets to automatically turn on the lights, turn up the heat, crank up the stereo and start supper—all so it's less lonely when he gets home! Sometimes we cope by overworking, overspending, overeating or watching TV. The lives and relationships of soap opera characters entice and titillate, pushing loneliness aside—at least for that hour.

What Is Loneliness?

If we want to bloom in relationships, we need to keep loneliness to a manageable size. Loneliness wears different faces, depending on your stage in life. For the one-year-old, loneliness is the huge gap between the safety of the coffee table and Daddy's waiting hands!

For the three-year-old, watching big sister board the school bus for the first time prompts tears: "Who will I play with?" And in middle-age, you tear open a birthday card from your son and discover no letter enclosed—that's loneliness! Or it might be having no one to call on the phone, like Bobby Vinton's "Mr. Lonely."

Loneliness is a fact of life for even the most flitty gadabout. So we're better off when we learn to deal with it. Each of us *has* to be alone at times—life can't be a constant whirl of parties, eating out and shopping.

In fact, sociologists and psychologists tell us that being alone is the most *common* human condition. At most of life's difficult transitions, you go it alone. At the beginning of life, the baby leaves the comfort of the womb to enter the stark delivery room—alone. At the end of life, each of us crosses the threshold of death alone.

Even in close relationships, there is a realm where you are alone with your private thoughts, histories and hopes. No one else truly knows how *your* grief feels, how much your promotion means, where your marriage is succeeding or failing, what your pain does to you.

So why do we fear aloneness so much that we avoid it at all costs, surrounding ourselves with people in a mad rush to do *something*, anything? I think it's safe to say that most of us would be happier if we'd just learn to handle being alone.

The events and experiences that make us lonely depend on our perspective and past. An autumn leaf floats lazily to the street—does that make you feel lonely? Is it a reminder that summer is past and you aren't getting any younger? Or is it heartwarming, bringing back the sniff of burning leaves and toasting marshmallows?

Our attitudes play a major role in how we view life. Curling up with a book in an empty house means coziness to one person, social failure to the next.

You might start some interesting conversations by asking people what loneliness means to them. You'll probably hear answers like "showing up at a party in T-shirt and jeans when everyone else has black ties," or "being the only kid on the block without roller skates." Such definitions usually tell something about the person giving them—like, "*I* was the kid who didn't have roller skates, and did I ever hate my parents for a while!" Feeling lonely brings emotional pain. That may seem obvious, but it helps explain why we avoid loneliness so desperately. It causes *pain*!

Lonely Circumstances

Sometimes we confuse loneliness with rejection, with not having any friends. But we can sit in the middle of a room teeming with friends or co-workers and still feel lonely. It doesn't matter how many friends we actually have; loneliness strikes when we *think* no one else cares.

In the book *Loneliness: Living Between the Times*, Nancy Potts offers the example of Katie, a woman who attends a small church where the service usually closes with everyone joining hands in a circle. Katie wrote the following note to the minister one week: "Thank you for ending the service by having the congregation hold hands. I live a very lonely life, and Sunday . . . is the only time I'm touched by another person all week."[1]

Like Katie, we can be lonely because of circumstances rather than because no one likes us. (Katie's story also tells

---

[1]Nancy Potts, *Loneliness: Living Between the Times* (Wheaton, Ill.: Victor Books, 1978), p. 40.

me that people who live alone need human touch!)

Some circumstances we count on to trigger loneliness—moving to a new town, or losing a spouse. One counselor suggests that even happy events can cause a surge of emptiness. You finally get your dream house, then suddenly realize it doesn't solve all your problems. Or your daughter's first date puts a lump in your throat. You're proud to see her grow up, but you also know she has to make her own choices. A birthday, job change, being in a position of leadership—all of these can make you feel unexpectedly lonely.[2]

Learning what causes our lonely feelings can be the key to eliminating them. Is there a pattern?

My folks and relatives all live some distance away, and I know I always feel depressed when they pull out of our driveway after a visit. I try to do something special the day they leave, like having a lunch date with a friend.

Sometimes we cause our own loneliness. We cut ourselves off from others, perhaps unwittingly. Shyness and loneliness often go together. A person who seems "stuck up" or proud may actually suffer from an acute case of shyness *and* loneliness!

Deepest Despair

Facing a terminal illness is the loneliest situation I can imagine. Friends and families may surround and sympathize, and even offer company twenty-four hours a day. But only the one who is sick can possibly know the inner isolation that accompanies the thought of dying.

Does faith provide answers for this kind of loneliness? Not necessarily. Doris Janzen Longacre, a woman dying of cancer at thirty-nine, explained it this way in a sermon: Faith in God didn't provide an answer to the suffering and loneliness, but it did provide a presence—a knowledge that

---

[2]Ibid., pp. 22–23.

God is stronger, more loving and wiser than we can understand. God's presence is really the only comfort for many of life's lonely times.

On the flip side, those who lose a loved one are also plunged into profound loneliness. Heartache and pain of loss afflicts survivors as surely as any illness; for survivors, the chief cure is time.

A certain amount of busyness, such as starting a new hobby or joining a club, can be a good remedy. So can avoiding situations that cause you loneliness. If looking at photo albums causes pain, put them away for a while. If Sunday afternoons are especially lonely, invite others over for dinner and an afternoon of conversation or games. What if you don't feel up to inviting company? Eat out with a friend or relative. You might feel you can't afford it, but it's cheaper than therapy!

The best counsel I've heard is to do what works best for *you.* Potts tells the story of a woman who received a number of letters from well-meaning friends after her husband's death. One said, "If it were me, I'd stay sedated until the shock wore off. Then I'd face life gradually, as I could handle it." Then the next letter came: "Don't let anyone sedate you. The sooner you face reality, the better."

Or sample these two gems: "Take it from one who has been there. Get back to work as quickly as possible. Staying busy keeps your mind off your sorrow." The next letter: "If I were you, I'd take a vacation and get some rest. But don't spend the time with relatives; they'll only accent the pain." Still another letter said: "Take some time off and visit relatives. They'll understand and be able to support you through this."

And finally, there were these two letters: "Whatever you do, sell your house. Memories will kill you." And the opposite: "I hope you can remain in your house. You and Jack shared so much of your lives there."[3] Priceless letters!

---

[3] Ibid., pp. 83–84.

Confronting Our Loneliness

Whatever the source of our loneliness, all of us are less lonely when we forge good relationships on the job, with family, at church, with neighbors or old friends. Even when you don't feel like taking the first step in a relationship, do it anyway. If you get to the place where you really can't take that first step—where you're emotionally incapable of reaching out—get some professional help. Loneliness and depression often go hand-in-hand, so counseling can be helpful.

What else helps curb loneliness? Doing something worthwhile for someone else. "Adopt" a grandfather or grandmother, or a little brother or sister.

Spending time in meditation with God can also ease loneliness. We were made to live in fellowship with our Creator. Use times of aloneness for reflection and journaling. Many stirring pieces of writing—glimpses of God's steadfast presence—have come out of dark moments of the soul. God won't necessarily take away the loneliness, but He will help you survive it and grow in strength and maturity. Spending time with Him will help to eclipse the loneliness. God doesn't want us to suffer from loneliness. He created us to enjoy fellowship with Him and others. When we despair, He is as grieved as any parent who sees his child suffering. None of us are immune from loneliness, but at least we can gain character through our suffering.

Even Jesus suffered deep alienation. We usually think of the time when the disciples fell asleep in the Garden of Gethsemane as Jesus' loneliest hour. They deserted Him, failing to pray when He most needed them. But from the very beginning of Christ's ministry we see moments that were clearly painful and alone, such as His wilderness experience and temptation, and His disciples' misunderstandings ("Don't you know or understand *yet*?" we hear Him asking the disciples. "Are your minds *so dull*. . . ?"—Mark 8:14–21, TEV). Even Christ's earthly family misunderstood

His ministry and wanted to redirect it: "When his family heard about this, they set out to get him, because people were saying, 'He's gone mad!' " (Mark 3:21).

But ultimately, it was estrangement from His heavenly Father that cut deepest. Jesus cried from the cross, "My God, why have you *forsaken* me?" (Matt. 27:46). Like Christ, we are not immune from the pain of loneliness. But trust in God helps us overcome.

Finally, believe the truism that *time* helps heal the hurts that cause loneliness. People who've suffered in many circumstances confirm that again and again. Healing takes longer for some, and scars persist. Time provides distance and perspective so that hurt fades and loneliness subsides. In a perfect world, there would be no loneliness, only aloneness when we wanted it. This isn't a perfect world, so we cope the best we can. We take comfort in knowing that loneliness is part of our human condition, and also in knowing that moments of fellowship and true friendship are part of the divine plan.

Specific Tips:

1. Analyze what provokes lonely feelings in you. List three times you've felt especially lonely.

2. What cheers you up? List some possibilities.

3. Think of someone you know who may be lonely. Arrange a visit.

HOW TO GET ALONG WITH THE PEOPLE WE LOVE MOST

CHAPTER SIXTEEN

I was called away on a business trip on short notice. It was only a one-night trip, so child care wasn't too difficult to arrange. Even during such a short trip I found myself missing the children and fantasizing how wonderful it would be to have them run headlong into my arms on my return.

Well, the homecoming may have happened like that, but all too soon three children were clamoring for me to see this picture, and to get the scissors, and to fix supper. The people who took care of the kids reported that they were really good while I was gone. So why do they turn into incredible little monsters for me, the mother they profess to love so much, almost immediately after I get home?

I knew it was normal behavior because I've seen it happen with other parents and children. And on second thought, maybe I do the same thing: at the office, glowing and sweet and patient and kind, even under intense pressure—and ten minutes later at home, snarling like a pit-bull dog.

Home is the place where it's safe to let our shirts hang out—children and adults alike. Unfortunately, home is also the abode of the people we love most—so we need to be aware how easily loving relationships can be damaged at home. How terrible it would be to "gain the whole world in friendship and lose our own family"! Family members are our first and last friends, but sometimes we treat them with as much consideration as our worst enemies.

This chapter will focus primarily on the relationship between husband and wife. For many of us, marriage is the longest, most intimate relationship we will ever experience. Even our relationships with our children should play second fiddle to friendship with a spouse.

Marriage

To what other friendship have you made "till death do us part" vows? Most friendships don't survive the intense differences of opinion, the daily annoyances, the staggering crises that most marriages go through. So when we toast 5, 10, 15, 25 years of marriage and more, we really do have something worth celebrating.

Unfortunately, our society romanticizes marriage as a "be-all." We expect it to fulfill all our needs for companionship and to "make" us happy. We dream that a good relationship will come as easily as the mythical state called "falling in love." The reality of marriage just can't stack up to our romantic ideals. And so when our days become routine or rough, we wonder if we've made a big mistake.

Marriage is one of the wonderful gifts God gave to us as humans. A good marriage provides a natural environment for daily companionship. The beauty of sharing experiences and feelings over the years is hard to put into words. It becomes a kind of spiritual/emotional/physical bond. I know of couples who experimented with trial separations only to realize that they had come through too much to leave each other. Their heads and hearts belonged together.

Every marriage has up-and-down cycles. As humans we fail and make mistakes that result in alienation. Yet bad times can be phases that help shape up some aspect of the relationship. Only when partners are unwilling to grow and change is there real difficulty.

Good sex, having children, growing a garden, painting and fixing up an old tumble-down house, pacing the floor of the emergency room together, celebrating Christmas and holidays—these are some of the things marriage partners walk through together, learning to help each other get through the misunderstandings and down times. The continual nurturing with love is what helps each person to grow and weather the hard times.

Think of a houseplant. It has two basic requirements, sun and water. Some plants take more and others less; some can live through lengths of neglect. But all plants do best if they receive regular, consistent care. Moreover, some plants need the almost constant caring hands of a real plant lover.

Marriage is the kind of plant that needs constant care. We need to be marriage "lovers"! That is, we need to cherish the marriage relationship enough to give it the regular attention and care it needs. The relationship may be able to exist or maintain on sporadic attention. But it will only thrive and bloom with that extra touch.

Caring for Your Marriage

How can you nurture your marriage? Well, if the basic requirements of houseplants are sunshine and water, perhaps we could say that the basics for your marriage are communication and commitment. Without both, your marriage will soon look as sad as a houseplant you neglected for three months.

But communication is an over-used word. It belongs to the advertisers and corporations and technology. Communication between a husband and wife goes beyond talking to include whispering and laughing, private jokes and back-rubs. In other words, gestures and unspoken messages say as much as words! Stony silences and times when no words will come are also communication.

Commitment is the "want-to" that drives a marriage. Sometimes we lose sight of this "want-to" in the daily hassles of car break-downs and burnt roasts and clashing schedules. We can go for days, even weeks and months, without giving too much thought to the condition of our marriage.

But then a crisis—losing a job or a child becoming ill—might make us aware that we haven't been thinking much about each other. Or it might be the *lack* of a crisis that prompts you to think about your marriage. Where's the old spark? Even when you argue you don't seem to care what happens.

Close relationships bring out either the best or the worst in us. When we work with men and women on the job, we have to find ways to work in harmony. Sometimes that takes a lot of effort. But if we're committed to staying on that job, it's what must be done. Marriage takes the same work and commitment, only more so.

Let's go back to our houseplant: just as a houseplant needs an occasional shot of fertilizer or plant food to really flourish, so marriage needs an occasional zap of energy.

One boost may be your *other* relationships. "We are seeing more and more couples suffering from an overexposure to each other," one marriage counselor says. "The bubbles of early wedded joy have gone flat, and they are tired of TV. One helpful way to maintain vitality in a marriage is private friendships—good friendships can actually strengthen a marriage. If you have a friend, you feel nicer about yourself and are easier to love."[1]

Other shots-in-the-arm include a short vacation trip or a special project you both want to work on. One woman was delighted when she and her husband discovered a common

---

[1]Carol Saline, "Why Can't Married Women Have Men As Friends?" *McCall's*, January 1975, p. 67.

interest in their family histories. "Now we have something to do *together*," she explained. Even something as simple as reading a book that moves you closer to your spouse can make a difference in your relationship.

The key through all is prayer, for your own marriage as well as those of your children or friends. One mother suffered with her son through the breakup of his ten-year-old marriage. Her other children's marriages are going fine, but she says she's realized in a new way the importance of praying for these already healthy marriages. After a divorce it's a little late to start praying for a marriage.

Just another note. By praying for your own marriage I don't mean asking God to change the other person. One man testified how his marriage soared once he stopped telling God how his wife needed to get more done around the house. Things went better only after he asked God to help him see where *he* could help.

A happy marriage may look bland, a bit unexciting from the outside. Maybe that's why we hear more about unhappy and broken marriages than we do about successful ones. As one writer pointed out, we frequently hear that over one-third of all marriages break up. But we don't often hear another statistic: Well over two-thirds of all first marriages endure. Second and third marriages swell the divorce statistics, hiding the fact that happy marriages occur all around us.

What benefits can we expect from working for a good marriage relationship? Companionship rather than mere co-existence. Ability to serve and know God together. A sense of purpose for your life as a person *and* as a couple. Better feelings about yourself as a person. Healthy marriages build self-worth, while a split up usually causes self-doubts. Every ounce of energy you invest in improving your marriage is worth it.

Marriage also provides a refuge, a place to be refueled. We can build each other up. We can team together in time, money and skills for reaching out to others.

Lastly, one of the rewards of working toward a good marriage is the feeling of having truly *lived*—of loving and being vulnerable to hurt and loss and growing in the discipline of caring. In some ways, I think it would have been easier to remain single than to risk rejection, failure, being hurt. The act of marriage is taking a dare!

The vulnerability we experience in marriage can help us be more open in other relationships. Losing is always a part of loving—experiencing loss at death, or the hurt of being misunderstood or seeing a friend move away. But without these experiences, painful though they are, we do not truly live.

The Rest of the Family

How are we around the rest of the family? Do we treat our children at least as well as we do our friends? If we recorded our conversation at the dinner table, what would we sound like?

Peg and Joe are parents of two teenagers. One evening after supper Joe took Peg aside and said, "Do you realize what you sounded like tonight?"

"No, what do you mean?" she asked.

"Well, first you asked why Donnie hadn't combed his hair since basketball practice. Then you asked Jeanine why she still had her good sweater on. And when Jeanine said she was full after a modest helping of casserole, you complained that she looked anorexic, and that she'd better start eating more. Next you jumped all over me for using too much salt," Joe smiled sympathetically.

Peg obviously wasn't much fun to eat with. But she was unaware of the tension she was causing. Even if all her complaints were legitimate, airing them in a different setting would be more considerate of her family.

Roommates

Consider Sue and Tina who've shared an apartment for almost a year. "If she picks up my paper one more time before I'm through with it," Sue says through gritted teeth, "I'm leaving!"

Tina's side of the story? "Before we moved in together, I thought Sue was the most fun person to be around. But now all I see is the mess she makes. I never mention it because I think, well, we'll only be in this apartment a year together. And I can stand anything for a year."

Tina's approach may smooth things on the surface, but if Tina learned how to express her concerns she might find Sue fun to be around. I guess that's a fundamental of friendship: a true friend knows how to give and take in a conflict, how to communicate clearly and how to listen with love. The beauty queen with the plastic smile may win the popularity contest, but I'd rather be around someone who lets me behind that painted face.

It takes time to move past superficial relationships. Likeable people take time for the people in their lives, including the ones at home. It's difficult to really communicate when we make home a sandwich shop where we pop in just to eat and zoom out to attend another meeting. It's hard for children to have fun with their parents when each day consists of meeting the school bus, hurrying to sports practice and then rushing off to piano lessons. Every family feels governed by impossible schedules. But somewhere in a busy week there must be time for each other.

Helen and Ken lead active lives. But while the children were small they made Saturday morning their family time. There was no cartoon-watching. After enjoying a leisurely breakfast in bathrobes, they played games, read, or listened to music. I envy their family tradition!

Set appointments if you need to in order to get the family together. Learn to keep your promised meeting times even when other things press in. (Even business associates will usually accept a firm but gracious "I can't come that night. I already have an appointment.") Decide together what family times are inviolable. Some families have rules about no meetings or clubs on birthday nights.

TV steals family time. It's one thing to purposely sit down together to watch and discuss a show, quite another to watch without forethought, or while trying to play a game or hold a discussion. For married couples, a TV in the bedroom is often a big mistake. Invariably one partner falls asleep too early, and the other wants to keep watching a show too late.

We make time for the things that are truly important to us. And the people we love most deserve our best.

Specific Tips:

1. Make an ongoing mental commitment to work at closeness. This week make a date with your spouse or plan times with the children.

2. Do something nice for each member of your family this week. Try to make it something unexpected, and try to do it anonymously.

3. If you sense that a family member needs "space" instead of closeness, list two ways you can give him or her that space. Then follow through!

4. Talk about your differing needs as a family. Let each member complete this sentence: "What I need/want most from my family right now is . . ."

5. Tape-record a conversation at mealtime to see how you all sound. Play it back when everyone is in a good mood.

HOW TO GET ALONG WITH YOUR WORST ENEMY

CHAPTER SEVENTEEN

Throughout most of this book I've been describing "beautiful" people—those so charismatic that you can't help but like them and the traits that make them that way. But perhaps the true test of a person's beauty is how well he or she gets along with difficult people.

One of life's hardest tasks is learning to accept an obnoxious, self-centered, irritating or otherwise difficult person: Why does he always interrupt people? Why doesn't she *listen* to me once in a while? Why does he think he's the center of the universe? Why doesn't she care about anyone else?

Misfit

A friend told me about a little girl named Alma. Alma's mother, Greta, was a strange combination. She looked beautiful, and she always dressed Alma in the prettiest dresses, but she wasn't *kind*. She never listened to Alma. She literally pushed her, because Alma couldn't walk fast enough. Greta pushed the rest of the family too. Her husband never made enough money; her children never earned high enough grades or worked hard enough; and her friends could never meet her high standards.

As a child, Greta had been the misfit in a family of three beautiful girls. She had never felt loved or accepted. Throughout her childhood, she drove herself just as she now drove every member of her family.

Coping with difficult people in a one-time encounter is trying but manageable. Dealing with them in a long-term relationship can be next to impossible.

Each of us has personal patterns of behavior. In the book *Coping With Difficult People*, Dr. Paul Schmidt says that a person's "habitual way of seeing the world, coping with emotions, and relating to people" can be called a person's "character style."[1]

Some people actually have what can be called "character disorders." A person with a character disorder doesn't necessarily show signs of a major mental disorder. Let me repeat: A character disorder is *not* something that is dangerous, or a threat to society, or a mental or medical disease. It is a person's characteristic way of thinking and relating. This character style grows out of their own life experience, so people with character disorders often feel perfectly good about themselves. It's the rest of the world that has problems.[2]

Usually, the difficult person's pattern of relating in some way *protects* him or her from close personal relationships. "I just can't seem to get close to him" is a typical response to a difficult person.

No Guarantees

In her well-known book *Irregular People*, Joyce Landorf tells story after story of people suffering hurt and rejection

---

[1]Paul F. Schmidt, *Coping With Difficult People* (Philadelphia: Westminster Press, 1980), p. 13.
[2]Ibid., p. 14.

in their families—rejection which often began in childhood. She borrows the term "irregular" from the book and movie *The Summer of My German Soldier*. The story describes a young girl cruelly abused and rejected by her father. When this young girl asks a favorite older friend why her mother ever married her father, the friend replies: "When I goes shopping and I sees something marked 'irregular,' I knows that I ain't gonna have to pay so much for it. Girl, you got yourself some irregular folks, and you've been paying top-dollar for them all along."[3]

Landorf tells how a mother adored her first-born daughter and didn't want any more children. She felt complete. But the father wanted more, and the second daughter was adored by the father. This woman wrote, "I do not ever remember my mother dressing me or combing my hair or bathing me."[4]

Then Landorf describes a young woman who had just discovered she had breast cancer. She was scheduled for surgery, and even though she had never really been able to talk with her mother, she felt her mother would have to listen because of the seriousness of her situation. As they drove home from a lunch date, the daughter spilled her story.

There was silence. The daughter asked her mother if she'd heard, if she understood. The mother nodded her head, then changed the subject: "You know, your sister has the best enchilada recipe. I'll have to give it to you." Of course, the mother was just trying to deny reality. But to the daughter, this response seemed utterly cold and uncaring.

Do you think these are isolated horror stories? Perhaps they're extreme, but if you talk to friends and relatives you'll find that most people either have someone in their family or know someone who can rightly be termed "difficult." Of-

---

[3]Joyce Landorf, *Irregular People* (Waco: Word Books, 1983), p. 24.
[4]Ibid., p. 33.

tentimes, the person is hard to live with in part because of childhood experiences.

Therapists who deal with people with character disorders say many of them had some crippling experience in their childhood. This, in effect, handicaps them. While it's true that everyone is free to make choices and to change, it's also hard to erase years of rejection or disappointment.

Difficult persons may have received plenty of discipline, instruction and correction, but little affirmation. These people have an unsatisfied hunger for affirmation. It's amazing that they achieve any sort of healthy adulthood. They survive, but with an emotional handicap as severe as if a childhood accident had claimed their sight, hearing or mind.

Irregular people somehow don't fit normal patterns of thinking, talking, behaving, giving and receiving love. Long ago I remember hearing a woman talk about Luke, a man in her church. It didn't matter what a group discussed, Luke was always on a different wavelength. Peg especially found him difficult to deal with. It was amazing they could both agree on membership in the same church when they felt as differently about everything as they did! And, indeed, Peg knew her bad feelings toward Luke couldn't continue if she was to stay at that church.

She prayed for forgiveness and a changed attitude, but it didn't happen automatically. She began to focus on his good points. He was unquestionably loyal to his wife and to the church. He was a hard worker, and contributed generously both with time and money. It took literally *years* of praying for a more accepting attitude before Peg finally felt genuine love for this difficult person. They still didn't agree on much, but eventually they could sit beside each other in worship!

Try to Understand

How do you cure a difficult person? Well, you don't. But there are ways to keep yourself from being manipulated.

Ask yourself how the person gets to you. Do you try to ignore his behavior, then suddenly explode? Why do you feel threatened? Or why does that person bring out your worst side? What can you do to avoid potential strife?

Being sensitive to traits typical of difficult people can also help you deal with them. Communication commonly causes problems in relating to difficult people, because few difficult people have developed good "people skills." Bill, for example, is an interrupter. It's not only annoying to talk to him, but next to impossible to get your own point across. He tends to guess at what you're saying, and frequently jumps to faulty conclusions.

We also need to examine whether we make up part of the problem, and make appropriate changes. Believe it or not, sometimes you find that other people think *you're* difficult. At a meeting, I was introduced to Tillie, a woman I had heard of through a mutual friend but never met. Immediately I said, "Oh, I believe you know Ben Conway (not his real name). I work at the same office he does."

"Uh-oh," Tillie made a face. "Ben is a real thorn in my side. We've always locked horns."

Too late, I remembered that Ben thought the same thing about this woman. Since the feeling was mutual, I began to wonder who was *really* the difficult person!

When two people have trouble getting along, fault often lies with both. At other times blame actually does belong only to one person—sometimes, no matter how hard you try to reason with a person, or no matter what you do to show your love, you're continually misunderstood.

Finally, be understanding. If there is a difficult person in your life, consider the person's background. For example, Carl resented Aunt Betty's unsolicited advice on raising children, especially because she didn't have any of her own. But once Carl learned how she had tried for years to have children, he began to understand her deep love for the kids she corrected.

Try to discover all you can about the person's growing-up years. Was he or she rich or poor? Popular or lonely? Was school easy or hard? You don't have to be a psychologist to recognize that a child who lost his parents at an early age, or who experienced extreme poverty or suffering might have had some problems growing up—and may still have some now.

A parent may be emotionally blind to one child while accepting of another. I'm not talking about a simple case of imagined favoritism, a "Mother-liked-you-best" syndrome that has little basis in fact. I'm referring to repeated snubbings, denials and mistreatment over the years.

In Coleen McCullough's *Thornbirds*, little Megan helps her mother diligently with chores, trying so hard to please her but never receiving any approval or recognition. Most of the mother's affection went to her first-born son, a love-child from a broken romance. Megan almost falls into the same pattern as she grows older and has children of her own, focusing most of her attention and love on her son rather than her daughter. But in the end she realizes how devastating such blindness has been in her own life. The heartbreaking thing is that children often grow up to have the same blind spots their parents have.

To be honest, most of us are difficult at one time or another. Moreover, some famous, influential people were probably considered "difficult" by their relatives. Think about Peter, for example, the disciple of Jesus. He was so impulsive that he tried to walk on water and he cut off a man's ear. Three times he loudly denied that he knew Christ. But God used Peter as a witness to multitudes, and Jesus pronounced Peter a "rock" upon which he would found the Church (Matt. 16:18). We all have quirks that make us hard to live with—and so we should be slow to point fingers and judge.

Accepting difficult people isn't easy. Sometimes we have to set a limit on the length of time we will spend with that person. Do I have the energy to endure a long evening together? It's easy to look down on the person difficult to be around. But in God's eyes, that person is as worthy as we are.

And that's what coping with difficult people is really all about. We usually can't change another person's habits. But we can seek to accept that person as a human being, a person of worth and dignity. Like the old saying goes, "There's so much good in the worst of us, and so much bad in the best of us that it behooves all of us not to talk about any of the rest of us!"

Specific Tips:

1. Pray daily for a difficult person you know. Pray also for yourself and your attitudes.

2. Joyce Landorf suggests that it's best *not* to have unrealistic expectations that things will suddenly improve. If you're anticipating a gathering where your difficult person will be present, don't build up hope for a storybook get-together.

3. Try to understand the person's personality and background. Ask an older, sensitive relative about the person's growing-up years. If you know specifically what sets him or her off—like your pets jumping on his clothes, or loud family discussions—try to keep these under control. See if there is any pattern to your problems together.

4. If a blowup occurs, forgive, forget and apologize. But recognize that you may receive none of this in return. For Christians, it's important to keep forgiving the other person *and* yourself so that healing can occur and a normal life go on.

5. Remember: Life *does* go on. Don't let a difficult person ruin it for you. For every thorn in your life, think of the people who make your life easier, better, more enjoyable.

WHY IT'S OKAY TO BE UNLIKEABLE AT TIMES

CHAPTER EIGHTEEN

Regarding an actor renowned for his boyishness, the authors of a *Ladies' Home Journal* article wrote, "There are problems that come with being a boy who never grew up, but such people can be the most delightful, enjoyable companions."[1]

If childishness is the price of being liked, I guess I'll pass on popularity. Certainly, we all know that the best life doesn't consist of endless enjoyment. Life isn't a game of *Trivial Pursuit*.

Life consists of serious issues and questions. There are tragic setbacks that must be confronted—not joked away. I can't imagine anything more boring than having all my relationships fun to the point of frivolity.

One of my life's most freeing moments came when I realized God probably didn't mean for me to be as outgoing as a friend of mine. *And that was okay!* A writer works mostly in solitude, away from the company of others. A teacher, on the other hand, couldn't do her work in solitude. God outfitted me with the personality best suited for my

---

[1] *Ladies' Home Journal*, August 1986, p. 139.

vocational gifts. (Or perhaps it works the other way around: I chose a vocation which suits my personality!) At any rate, it's the same with my friend, and *the same with every human being*: We are most free when we accept ourselves as we are.

But beyond these basic differences in personalities, being always-and-forever-100-percent-super-likeable isn't always a virtue. We don't want to be pushovers.

We don't want to be abrasive either. Are you uncomfortable being told you should be more assertive? "Don't let people walk all over you!" advises your friend. Books and magazine articles proclaim: "Get what you want! Tell people how you feel!"

It's good to learn techniques that help us more honestly reveal what we're feeling and wanting from relationships. But many of us feel discomfort at the command to "be assertive." It seems to ignore other people's needs. Is there any way two people can *both* have their own way?

Assertive or Aggressive?

There *is* a difference between assertive and aggressive behavior, say David Augsburger and John Faul in a book called *Beyond Assertiveness*. Assertiveness stands up for legitimate rights without violating the rights of others, maintaining love and respect for the other person.

Aggressive behavior, on the other hand, violates the rights of others in the process of claiming its own. Aggressive behavior dominates and humiliates.[2]

Learning assertiveness can be in everyone's best interest. When your friend calls and says she and her family are coming over for the evening, what do you do? You're caught off guard, and since you had only planned for a family evening of games and popcorn, you lamely say, "Yeah, sure. Come on over."

---

[2]John Faul and David Augsburger, *Beyond Assertiveness* (Waco: Calibre Books, 1980), p. 14.

But you're tired. You had really looked forward to just lounging with the family in your robe. You quickly tidy up the rooms and change clothes—all the while resenting it more and more that you didn't feel free to say it really wasn't okay. By the time they finally arrive, you've thought of a dozen reasons why they're inconsiderate and why you don't like their company. You've set yourself up for a miserable evening.

You could have said something like, "It would be nice to get together with your family soon. We'd enjoy that a lot. But I was really hoping to just unwind a bit tonight from a hectic week. How about if you come over next Friday night? We can have dinner together."

That would have expressed your needs without neglecting your friend's. You affirm their value to you. In the first instance, you not only feel angry about not getting to relax like you planned, but you begin to feel guilty for being angry. You get mad at yourself for your selfishness, and think, "I'm really a rotten person to not want to share this evening with my friend and her family!"

Augsburger and Faul point out that love "tempers the sharp edge of assertiveness."[3] A weekend's training program won't make you a loving, assertive person. The ideal assertiveness training program promotes self-understanding and self-appreciation *along with* an equal interest in appreciating and understanding others.[4]

This matches my understanding of what Scripture teaches us about love. In 1 Cor. 13:4–7, we see that "love is patient and kind; . . . it is not arrogant or rude. Love does not insist on its own way. . . . Love bears all things, believes all things, hopes all things, endures all things." It's no wonder that many of us feel uncomfortable around aggressive people who demand their own way to the point of being rude.

---

[3]Ibid.
[4]Ibid.

It *is* possible—although sometimes tricky—to be assertive yet respect other people. I can still be supportive and affirming without lying down like a doormat. When we let people use us, we only perpetuate the problem, and our relationships suffer as a result.

Test your assertiveness quotient: How many times a day do you say something like, "I know this isn't important, but . . ." or "This is probably a stupid question, but . . ."

I use those phrases too much, even though I know there are no stupid questions. Even if something is important just to me, then it's important.

Manipulative

When we're not straightforward about what we want, sometimes we use indirect, manipulative methods. In the process, we not only lose our self-respect, but we place an unnecessary strain on our relationships.

A simple example of this: You make a delicious supper for your family. As they hurry to meetings and ball games, everyone forgets to say thank you. You can say nothing, then give them the silent treatment all evening, hoping that someone will guess why you feel taken for granted. Or you can express your need for affirmation: "Hey, I feel lousy when no one remembers to say thanks." This will clear the air, and you can get on with your evening instead of letting a simple oversight make you angry. Being assertive won't necessarily produce a thank you for every meal you serve, but it can help you feel better about yourself.

Sometimes we're scared to be assertive because we focus only on possible negative consequences. Karla never disagreed with her boss because she feared he would think she was an aggressive troublemaker. What she didn't see was that he might *also* notice that she had a mind of her own, that she had good ideas and that she might deserve a promotion.

I've found that when I act with a proper amount of self-confidence, people respond to me in a similar way. It's a bit like Christ's golden rule: If I treat myself with respect, others treat me with respect also. The right kind of assertiveness doesn't have to be pushy. It can even foster better understanding between people at the same time that it furthers what is right and good.

Specific Tips:

1. If you don't know if you're assertive, nonassertive, or aggressive, test yourself with this example: You're treated rudely by a waiter in a good restaurant. He takes forever to wait on you, mixes up your order, and then brings you blue cheese dressing instead of French. Do you:

a. Use the blue cheese and simply resolve not to give him a tip.

b. Make a big scene and demand to see the manager.

c. Tell him firmly that you really would like French dressing instead of blue cheese.

There are no right or wrong answers, but if you said you would use the dressing he brought and not give him a tip, you've responded *nonassertively*. Demanding to see the manager would of course be fairly *aggressive* in light of the nature of the incident; and asking him politely to bring the French dressing would be an *assertive* response: you get what you want without endangering his job.

2. Try listing all the areas in your life in which you would like to be more assertive.

Second, list the ways in which you are too assertive—perhaps at times you come on too strong.

Third, list the areas in which you feel your assertiveness is proper. For instance, you find you can be fairly assertive with your children but not with your mother-in-law. What do these clues tell you about yourself?

3. Try to state your needs in a loving way in one situation

this week. Then reflect on how you felt. Was it as bad as you expected? Were the results what you wanted, or did you at least reach an acceptable compromise? Did you lose your control and become aggressive or demanding?

PAIN IS A TEACHER (WE'D RATHER NOT HAVE)

CHAPTER NINETEEN

I had just finished the first draft of the manuscript for this book and prepared it for mailing to the publisher. Sweet freedom! I felt like a high schooler at the end of the semester, all my exams and papers finished. Of course I knew there would be editing and rewriting of it to do down the road, but at that point, I was free!

That night there was a knock on the door about 9:30. It was my husband, hobbling home early from his evening shift because he had fallen and hurt his knee. He'd been to the emergency room, and was to report to an orthopedic surgeon in the morning.

No big deal, we thought. "I'll try to come to work tomorrow evening," he told the supervisor who'd dropped him off.

The doctor had different ideas. He scheduled surgery for a torn ligament on December 31. I threw a pity party for myself that New Year's Eve, but my husband and I still thought, oh well, six weeks of recuperation at most. Weren't football players usually back on the field in three weeks?

I knew there were much, *much* worse crises than hurt legs, but that knowledge didn't help me much. There was wood to bring in, sidewalks to shovel, meals to make, bed-trays to carry, children to keep happy and dry, and a job to keep up. I had to wash, clean and help him with shampoos, bathing and dressing. A cast to the hip limited his movements severely, and at first he couldn't even get himself out of his chair. But the worst part was my running all the errands and doing all the chauffeuring. It seemed like I was constantly on the run and physically out of gas. Once the cast finally came off, it was another two months before my husband could gingerly start back to work.

That winter taught me I'd have some hard lessons to learn about life should a more severe crisis strike. When things are going well, most of us can be reasonably nice people. When life throws us a curve—if pain, disability or crisis comes our way—is it still possible to be our best in friendship?

No One Asks for Pain

When it comes to being thankful for pain, we're like the little girl who wrote her aunt a thank-you note for a birthday gift. The note said: "Dear Aunt Harriet, Thank you for the pin cushion you sent me for my birthday. I always wanted a pin cushion, but not very much."[1]

Well, we don't want pain very much either. It may help to remember that pain usually warns us that something's wrong. Think of how a heart attack victim may notice a tenderness or burning of skin on the left side of his chest. It's not the skin that's in danger, but the heart. The heart simply "borrows" the skin for a relay warning station, points out Philip Yancey in his excellent book on pain, *Where Is God When It Hurts?*[2]

---

[1] Ethel Barrett, quoted in *Baker's Pocket Book of Religious Quotes*, Albert M. Wells, Jr., Editor and Compiler (Grand Rapids, Mich.: Baker Book House, 1976).
[2] Philip Yancey, *Where Is God When It Hurts?* (Grand Rapids, Mich.: Zondervan Publishing House, 1977), p. 27.

Or think of leprosy patients. The danger of leprosy is that the patient doesn't feel pain. He cuts his foot and doesn't know it; by the time he finds the wound it's dirty and likely to become infected. Or he twists his ankle and tears a tendon, but doesn't feel it; he simply adjusts and walks crooked or crippled.[3] Life without pain would be dangerous for all of us!

These kinds of facts about my body help me realize that even though pain is uncomfortable, it's a valuable part of being human. It develops an ability within us to empathize, to relate to other people, to know how to help a hurting friend. It's as important a sense in my body as smell, sight, hearing and touch.

C. S. Lewis in his book *The Problem of Pain*[4] says that pain is a surgical procedure that frees us from selfishness and self-centeredness. Pain swiftly makes us aware of God's presence (or lack of it for the non-Christian). As we receive *God's* love, we become more loving.

No one illustrates this better for me than Mary Jane Detweiler, a woman who bears an extremely rare disorder called "transverse myelitis." An inflammation of the spinal cord, her illness causes a constant burning sensation—like a third-degree burn—over her entire body from her neck down. She's had it more than five *years*, including three major attacks of partial paralysis that forced her to learn to walk again.

Many, many times since I first met and talked to Mary Jane her pain has ministered to me. When I have a rough day or come down with the flu and a bad case of self-pity, she helps me put it all in perspective. She helps me have strength to become more of the person I want to be.

Pain teaches us what to say and what not to say to friends in pain. It teaches us how to be helpful, how to focus on

---

[3]Ibid., p. 32.
[4]C. S. Lewis, *The Problem of Pain* (MacMillan Company).

life's important issues. My limited experience with pain has shown me the beauty of friends and family pulling together to discover depths of love and caring that we're too harried to appreciate on ordinary days.

Specific Tips:

1. When someone you know is in pain, ask what his pain feels like and how he'd like you to pray.

2. Find a favorite hymn or psalm to read when feeling pain. Commit it to memory.

3. Think of a recent crisis or painful experience. How have you grown? What does it teach you about others in pain?

INGREDIENTS OF FRIENDSHIP

CHAPTER TWENTY

Della was a pastor's wife in the days when that was a career in itself. Always ready with a double recipe of casserole or soup for Sunday dinner, she spontaneously invited whatever visitors happened to be at church that day. If there were no visitors, she invited whoever didn't have their dinner already simmering in a crock pot. On arriving for the meal, Della's crew (her four children) and the guests were deftly drafted into service.

On a given Sunday, you might be asked to shred cabbage, pour drinks, or cut up peaches for dessert, so long as you didn't have little ones of your own to look after. With five- and eight-year-olds setting the table, the knives and spoons didn't always land on the right side of the plate, but the hospitality was real. I always felt like I could talk with Della about *anything*, and I frequently did. After her own children grew up, she and Peter began to keep foster children, so their household is still more or less child-proofed. There aren't many fancy do-nothings sitting around.

One summer I painted most of the rooms in their home. Working there every day for about two weeks, I found out that Della wasn't above losing her cool. She was like every other mother I've ever known. Not perfect—just human.

Ingredient #1: Comfortable Together

What makes her a friend to so many? An ad I saw for crystal made me think of Della. It said, "What good is having fine imported crystal if you're afraid to use it?" At Della's meals, you weren't afraid of breaking anything. While there *were* pretty things that you would have hated to break, somehow you knew she would never hold an accident against you. She made you feel *comfortable*.

Many people fear friendship, because to grow close to people we have to be vulnerable. People have to feel comfortable with us. And that means someone might reject our friendship and hurt us.

Ingredient #2: Time

Friendship takes time. One casualty of a two-career-plus-kids lifestyle is time for friends. No deep friendship was ever cultivated on a when-I-get-around-to-it basis. The details of living—work, children, housework—always consume our time unless we also make friendship a priority.

The late artist Georgia O'Keeffe once said, "[To really see a flower] takes time, like to have a friend takes time."[1] Preparing extra food for Sunday dinner takes time. Giving up quiet Sunday afternoons of reading, writing letters or napping to visit with friends takes personal time. Raising foster children after your own are grown takes lots of time.

Ingredient #3: Communication

Friendship also requires open communication—something we've examined over and over again because it's one of the most important keys to friendship. But in today's mobile society, people move so frequently that communication becomes difficult, if not impossible. Sometimes we

---

[1]Ad, *Washington Post* magazine, November 15, 1987, p. 54.

have to let go of old relationships. With those friendships, we make halfhearted stabs at keeping up old ties, saying, "We've just gotta get together sometime." Communication consists of a few scribbled lines on a Christmas card. I used to feel bad about the lapse of such friendships. But now I realize that life is meant to go on, moving us to new relationships with people closer to us.

A few special friendships withstand the test of time and moving away. When one old friend and I get together, we don't pretend things are the same as they always were, but try instead to catch up on what's happened to each other in the interim. When business or family travel makes it possible to get together, we make the special effort to meet. There's nothing like having a friend from the past who remembers how you looked in college, or how overjoyed you were at the prospect of a big date, or what your family was like when you were growing up.

Ingredient #4: Commitment

Friendship takes commitment. If time together and communication are to take place, it takes commitment to see it happen. Having a few good friends you can share with over a lifetime is important for wholeness.

Do you remember a time in childhood when your best friend suddenly became best friends with a more popular girl or boy? "But you were supposed to be my friend," says little Joanie, as if friendship could be demanded. One person can't hold a friendship together—no matter how much that person might want to. In the end, it takes two.

Ingredient #5: Initiative

A long-ago pen pal recently got in touch with me after more than a decade of not writing. She reminded me that "just like our relationship once began out of the blue" so it can be renewed out of the blue. The same goes for any relationship. A friendship can begin anytime and in an amazing variety of ways, but usually someone has to take the initiative. And that takes nerve.

I enjoy people, but sometimes it takes super-human effort for me to pick up the phone and say, "Why don't you come over tonight?" or to stop at a co-worker's desk and say, "Do you want to go out to lunch together today?" With practice it becomes easier and more natural, but it's easy to fear that people won't like us.

I was seated with my sister in a restaurant. She began to joke and laugh comfortably with the waitress, someone she really didn't know. As I envied her wonderful personality, I decided one of her gifts was initiative. I keep people at a distance until I'm sure they like me, while she invites them into her life *assuming* they'll like her. (How refreshing to know that when I feel inadequate, God loves me just the way I am, yet at the same time He nudges me to go further than I ever have before!)

It's important to distinguish, too, between the art of making *new* friends and that of keeping old ones. We can all think of people who are great meeters and mixers, but it is better to cultivate a few close friendships than to maintain many superficial acquaintances.

Community as Friendship

In Genesis we read that after God created Adam, He said, "It is not good for the man to be alone" (Gen. 2:18). Usually we think of that passage in connection with marriage, but surely it can be applied to all relationships. We were created to live in relationship with God and other humans, male and female.

It is this basic, divinely sparked need that tugs us toward community with other people. On the human side, we wear masks, recoil from criticism and allow shyness, anger or a disability to block communion with fellow human beings. As much as I crave aloneness for myself at times, I don't covet loneliness!

Christians don't have a corner on friendship; in fact, some mix "ministry" and friendship in a way that leaves a potential friend feeling used. If I only want the best for my friend—and if for me the best includes faith in Christ and belonging to a community of believers—then over the course of time, I hope to make Christianity and the Christian community attractive to my friend who's not so sure about Christ. (This, supplemented with faithful prayer, committed friendship and a large dose of God's grace!)

Long, long ago, I answered the question, "Do I want to be a Christian?" But only recently did I ask myself, "Why do I stay a Christian?" Because it's convenient? Comfortable? Because I want to avoid whatever I conceive hell to be? Do I stay in the church for my kids' sake, or to please my parents?

Perhaps a smattering of each of these enters into our never totally pure motives. But more and more, I've come to appreciate the community—fellowship, friendship, whatever you want to call it—that happens as believers join themselves together in relationships through Christ. Such a community transcends human frailties and everyday misunderstandings. In that community I can grow to become the best I can be in friendship and every area of my life.